THE SEASON OF YES

A GUIDE TO EMBRACING THE JOURNEY TO RETIREMENT JOY, PURPOSE, AND PROSPERITY

M. FELICIA DOUGLAS LITTLEJOHN,
IAR, NSSA®

It's Your Season of Yes!
Felicia D. Littlejohn

JT PUBLISHING HOUSE

THE SEASON OF YES

A Guide to Embracing the Journey to Retirement Joy, Purpose, and Prosperity

Names: Littlejohn, M. Felicia Douglas, author.
Title: The season of yes: a guide to embracing the journey to retirement, joy, purpose, and prosperity / M. Felicia Douglas Littlejohn, IAR, NSSA

Summary: "Retirement isn't a finish line. It's a season, and you get to say yes to it. You've spent decades saving, working, and planning for "someday." Now someday is here, and the questions have changed: How do I make my money last? When should I claim Social Security? How much will taxes really take? And, underneath all of that, what do I actually want the rest of my life to look like? The Season of Yes is a practical, warmly written roadmap through every stage of that transition, written by Felicia Littlejohn, a 20-plus-year investment advisor representative, licensed insurance agent, and National Social Security Advisor designee who has guided hundreds of families through retirement across the Carolinas and Georgia, and nationwide."— Provided by the author.

Subjects: BISAC: BUSINESS & ECONOMICS / Personal Finance / Retirement Planning | SELF-HELP / Aging | BUSINESS & ECONOMICS / Investments & Securities / General

Identifiers: ISBN 978-1-954624-41-2 (paperback)
ISBN 978-1-954624-42-9 (hardback)
ISBN 978-1-954624-43-6 (ebook)

Library of Congress Control Number: 2026947562

Printed in the United States of America

9 8 7 6 5 4 3 2

CONTENTS

DISCLOSURE

Felicia Littlejohn (registered as Margarette Felicia Craig, CRD #7189876) is an Investment Advisor Representative and is a licensed insurance agent in the states of South Carolina, North Carolina, and Georgia. Investment advisory services are offered through CreativeOne Wealth, LLC, a registered investment advisor. CreativeOne Wealth and Legacy Financial Advisors are not affiliated.

The contents of this book are provided for informational purposes only and are not intended to serve as the basis for any financial decisions. Any tax, legal, or estate planning information is general in nature. Please remember that converting an employer plan account to a Roth IRA is a taxable event. Increased taxable income from the Roth IRA conversion may have several consequences. Be sure to consult with a qualified tax advisor before making any decisions regarding your IRA. It should not be construed as legal or tax advice. Always consult an attorney or tax professional regarding the applicability of this information to your unique situation.

Information presented is believed to be factual and up to date, but we do not guarantee its accuracy, and it should not be regarded as a complete analysis of the subjects discussed. All expressions of opinion are those of the author as of the date of publication and are

DEDICATION

The foundation of transformational leadership is built on the principles ofunderstanding one's "what," "how," and "why." I know "what" I am: a registered investment adviser representative and servant leader.

My mother, Linda Sullivan, who lived a beautiful life, quintessentially enhanced and reinvigorated my "how" by encouraging me to transparently and passionately educate my clients on the complexities of managing their wealth and empowering them to help maximize their earning potential; to meet people where they are.

Thanks to the wisdom and guidance of my father, James C. Johnson, I know my "why," which is to intentionally and authentically lead, serve, and maintain the trust of my clients.

I believe my parents are chief angels and are in God's ear, making this experience happen. They've truly established the framework for me to become a leader who leverages my experience and goes beyond self-interest to help my clients experience seasons of "Yes."

PROLOGUE

Life has undergone a gamut of changes, introducing a new matrix of financial concerns and questions for embracing retirement joy, purpose, and prosperity for growing families, pre-retirees, and retirees.

In this much-needed book, author M. Felicia Douglas Littlejohn, IAR, NSSA, equips readers with dynamic, holistic strategies to help them navigate retirement for today and tomorrow. Mrs. Littlejohn targets the essential skills necessary for readers to succeed, such as the importance of creating a retirement dream, leveraging assets, relationships, and partnerships. At the heart of this book are real-life examples and insights tailored for diverse financial scenarios, including Lifetime Retirement Income, Tax Minimization, Social Security Benefits Maximization, vital Healthcare Planning, and so much more.

Timely, inspiring, and filled with Littlejohn's trademark professional, practical guidance, The *Season of Yes* will become a touchstone for individuals, business owners, women, and those seeking to create and embrace their retirement journey.

INTRODUCTION

WHERE PASSION MEETS PURPOSE

I remember that day so clearly—the day I learned that there was no money to pay for my college education. As the ninth of 13 children, I had watched several of my older siblings go through the process of talking to our dad about their college choices, about what they would major in, and how college would change their lives and put them on a path to success.

My Dad was always so proud of his ability to support his family, to help his children live out their dreams of building a better life for themselves. It's no small accomplishment to put several children through college, which he had succeeded in—and was planning to continue with the last three children. Like many other Americans, I am part of a blended family.

It was a beautiful fall morning, and I was getting ready for school, thinking about which college I wanted to go to and anticipating a new life filled with classes, friends, activities, and purpose. My Dad was getting ready for work, and we were talking as we had breakfast. "Daddy, I'm going to get ready to start applying for college," I told him.

"Baby girl, that's great!" he said. "You're so smart." But something was missing—there was no excitement or warmth in his voice.

Puzzled, I turned to look at him. Instead of an encouraging smile, he had a serious expression and seemed to be searching for the right words. My heart sank, but I didn't know exactly why—yet.

"Felicia," he finally said. "While you're planning on going to college, I'm having to start planning my retirement."

"What do you mean?" I asked. "I thought you wanted to keep working?"

"I do," he said. "But circumstances have changed. I can't keep working, which means that I need to retire. And so, I am not sure how I can help you with college."

"You mean I can't go to college?" I blurted out, shocked.

"No!" he replied with a dejected expression on his face. "I don't mean that. I can't pay for it like I was planning to."

Of all the things I expected to hear from my Dad, this was not one of them. I didn't really understand all the ins and outs of paying for college, how expensive it was, and if there were any other options for paying for it other than my Dad. What I did know was that I was set on going to college because I wanted to make a difference in the lives of others.

I hadn't always been so serious. In many ways, my life in a big family had unfolded in a predictable way. Because my older siblings were significantly older than me, I got to tag along on many of their adventures. I remember when my older brothers had dates and didn't want to bring me along, they would tell me they were going to the moon so I couldn't come. I enjoyed a pretty typical school life with friends and activities. I was always a good student.

What changed me was my brother's death. The middle of my siblings, Anthony, was a smart, talented, promising young man in his early 30s. We used to tease each other, listen to music, dance, and go together to the skating rink every Wednesday. We had the kind of close relationship that occurs within big families between two siblings who are living together and have kindred spirits. It was my habit to knock on his door in the early morning to help wake him up. for work. On that day, he didn't respond when I called his name, and when I went to shake him to wake him up, he seemed stiff. But I figured he was sleeping hard, and that he would wake up soon. In the meantime, I had to get ready for school, so I went back into my room to get dressed. In the busyness of getting myself ready, I forgot that he hadn't gotten up.

"Hey, Felicia, Anthony isn't up yet," my Dad said as we were getting ready to leave the house, him for work and me for school. We went to the other side of the house to wake him up, and he was still unresponsive. When I turned him over, we saw there was foam on his mouth. We looked at each other, dumbstruck. My father ran and called 911—remember, this was way before the cellphone era. Although the ambulance came quickly and the paramedics took great care, later at the hospital, my brother was pronounced dead.

The grief hit us all hard. Who could have imagined that a healthy, vital young man could die at such a young age? There was no understanding it, but ultimately, we had to accept that it was the Lord's will. Our faith helped pick us up and get back to a semblance of normal, even though my brother's absence couldn't be filled.

After my brother died, I became much more serious, much more focused. Instead of a carefree teenager, I became someone who was much more thoughtful, much more aware of life and how transient it was. My faith deepened, and what I wanted more than ever was a life of service, where I could really make a difference for others.

My brother, my other brothers and sisters, and I were all raised with the idea that life was about serving and helping others. My Dad used to quote the Gospel of Luke, saying, "For of those to whom much is given, much is required." After my brother's death, I understood service in an entirely different way. Service wasn't about helping others so that I could receive gratitude and praise in return—instead, it was about helping make their lives better because they mattered. They had problems, worries, and cares, just like me. And if I could do something to help them, that was the most meaningful activity I could engage in for my future.

Although it took longer than I thought—and a transfer back to a hometown college—I did graduate from college with a bachelor's degree in business management from the University of South Carolina in Spartanburg. My career led me to work in a law office, where I started using what I'd learned about finances and retirement to help people informally.

My pastor, noticing how skilled I was at helping others in this way, encouraged me to educate others in finances and retirement planning more formally, so I started offering seminars through my church, other churches, and organizations. What started out as a hobby—an opportunity to give back and share information to encourage others to get their affairs in order—became my vocation, and I started Legacy Financial Advisors, a financial planning firm with offices in Greenville and Anderson, South Carolina.

Today, my passion involves helping pre-retirees, retirees—and others—realize their dreams of building wealth, creating a unique retirement journey, and protecting their legacy for the benefit of their family and their communities. In this book, you'll gain an understanding of the techniques I use to help families throughout upstate South Carolina—and all over the country—thrive in retirement.

1

DISCOVERING YOUR RETIREMENT JOURNEY

What are your retirement dreams? As you prepare for retirement, you may not realize that retirement is not one fixed event in time, but a journey that occurs over time. For many people, that journey lasts 25, 30 or even 35 years—or longer.

Despite how frequently retirement occurs as more than 10,000 baby boomers retire every day, there is no one-size-fits-all retirement.[1] Your retirement journey is as unique as your other life experiences, and the experiences of your spouse. Understanding this fact about retirement, you need to consider what retirement will be like for you, and your spouse. Now is the time to take the proactive opportunity to shape your retirement now, while you have more options available to you.

To do that, you need to understand how you will spend your time once work, which occupied a significant part of your waking hours, isn't part of your life anymore. You need to reimagine your relation-

1. "10,000 Boomers Are Retiring Daily—How This Changes Banking and Your Finances," YahooFinance.com, June 2, 2024, https://finance.yahoo.com/news/10-000-boomers-retiring-daily-160054105.html

ships, where you will likely be spending much more time with your spouse than either of you are used to.

Retirement is also made up of several distinct phases, which some financial professionals have labeled as the go-go years, the slow-go years and the no-go years. During the go-go years, you're more active, engaging in the activities you may have missed while you were working. That might involve travel, babysitting your grandkids, starting a new hobby or something different.

The slow-go years, on the other hand, are when health concerns start to take a toll on your energy and mobility. Perhaps you still travel, but within the U.S. rather than overseas. You stay home more and enjoy the simple pleasures in life. The no-go years occur in the later years of retirement, when you may need more assistance in activities of daily living.

Retirement is the start of a new phase of your life. To fully capitalize on that opportunity and to get the most out of all the effort you've expended saving for retirement, you need to put some time and energy into imagining your retirement journey.

I'm Felicia Littlejohn, an investment advisor representative, licensed insurance agent and National Social Security Advisor designee. My mission is to help you discover your financial journey, plan for the future and live your best life. As the CEO and founder at Legacy Financial Advisors, (www.thelegacygroupsolutions.com) my passion comes from a personal challenging experience. Growing up in a large family, there weren't enough financial resources when it was my turn to go to college, creating a personal hardship. As a young adult, I realized that with proper financial planning years prior, this hardship could have been avoided.

This sparked my interest in all things financial and inspired me to build a comprehensive team of professionals to try to help others address their financial futures so that they can be better prepared to successfully meet their goals—like retiring with confidence, protecting wealth, and leaving a meaningful legacy.

My 20-plus years of experience guiding couples and individuals in South Carolina, North Carolina, Georgia and expanding nationwide, gave me the confidence to write this book to share strategies that pre-retirees and retirees can use to help position their finances for a sustainable retirement.

BIG PICTURE JOURNEY

As you've planned for retirement, your thoughts probably center on the financing side of retirement—have you saved enough money? Almost two-thirds of Americans surveyed by Allianz Life Insurance company worry they will run out of money when they aren't working anymore.[2] In another survey, a similar number said they aren't saving as much as they would like.[3]

Retirement, however, is much more than a retirement account and a checkbook. Retirement is a lifestyle, and one that represents a big change from how you've lived the rest of your adult life. If you're like most of my clients, you've worked your whole life. And you may have a hard time imagining what your life will be like without work.

You may identify retirement from that very vantage point—moving away from work, rather than moving towards a completely different lifestyle that you would pursue if you weren't too exhausted from working. If that sounds like you, don't feel bad, that's why you're reading this book. That's what we're here to talk about.

This is where it starts, though. What have you been putting off? How many times have you had to work on the first day of hunting season? How often have you looked longingly at your fishing boat as it collects cobwebs? What are the hobbies you have been nurturing that are actually your main passions in life? Because that's where we all have to start when we begin to truly plan for retirement. It's the

---

2. "Americans are More Worried About Running Out of Money than Death," Allianz Life Insurance Co., Apr. 22, 2025: https://www.allianzlife.com/about/newsroom/2025-Press-Releases/Americans-Are-More-Worried-About-Running-Out-of-Money-Than-Death.

3. "Americans are More Worried About Running Out of Money than Death," Allianz Life Insurance Co., Apr. 22, 2025: https://www.allianzlife.com/about/newsroom/2025-Press-Releases/Americans-Are-More-Worried-About-Running-Out-of-Money-Than-Death.

start of a journey that has the potential to be the best phase of a life well-lived.

For some people it means more work—many clients envision starting their own small business based on one of their passions that they had never had time to pursue, and this can be an incredibly rewarding way to supplement retirement income if—and only if—the passion is there first. In our practice, we have clients who pursue business ventures after they retire.

Here's a fictional example of how we might deal with this kind of situation: Kyle has an incredible passion for revitalization projects around the lakefront he owns property on, so much so that he brings it up at every meeting with his advisor. He's envisioning how he can improve the property, not just for himself, but to potentially develop other lakefront homes for people who want to slow down and enjoy a different pace of life.

Clearly, he has thought out his idea thoroughly, even to the point of talking to area developers and contractors. That's that kind of situation where I would encourage a sensible allocation of resources to live out his dream of retirement. The passion and knowledge for the business is already there and is worth pursing in retirement to bring that vision to life.

For other clients, they have a passion where it makes sense to participate in volunteer work, where they have a similar physical and social activity level to their work years but with reduced hours and stress. We work with these clients too, and here's another hypothetical example: A former elementary school teacher, Kathy, volunteers with the American Red Cross and the local Friends of the Library Association. She fills about half of her time with those activities, in addition to swimming at a local pool with a Master's Swimming Group. She competes in Master Swim Meets from time to time and also runs occasional programs for adult swimmers. These activities, and an active social circle, have kept her so busy during retirement that she now wonders how she had time to work!

And I would be hard-pressed not to mention travel, which is something that almost every retiree I meet with has dreams of doing.

Similarly, our practice has a lot of them as clients. As a hypothetical example of the kind of retiree we help: Sam and Susan enjoy biking, and they spent several weeks the year after they retired biking across Iowa with 30,000 other people during the 50th anniversary of RAGBRAI, the Des Moines Register's Annual Great Bike Ride Across Iowa in July 2023.[4] They also spent two weeks in Egypt and are planning a cross country camping trip with their dog to visit their daughter, who lives in Los Angeles.

For others still, it's the simplest of things—spending more time with family. Even though we aren't as young as we used to be and can have trouble keeping up with youngsters, they are a source of joy in our lives. I fondly remember an incident where my grandson ran out the front door of my house, and afraid that he would run into traffic, I ran after him. But I tripped and ended up rolling down the hill in the front of the house—and that actually stopped him, because he was laughing so hard at the sight of me rolling down the hill. Fortunately, it was a gentle hill, and I wasn't hurt! I've seen some situations where grandparents are so enamored with their grandchildren, that they move to where their kids are, so they can be more involved in their grandchildren's daily lives.

What it comes down to is figuring out what can give these years purpose. Nobody works hard for multiple decades to come to the other side of all that work and have no idea what will make them happy and fulfilled. Yet without the right plan this can and does happen.

I became motivated to help pre-retirees with retirement planning after seeing what happened to my Dad. He was forced to retire before he was ready, which left him in a difficult position. While there was enough income to maintain a lifestyle—barely—there was not enough to travel or fulfill potential bucket list dreams. My mother's retirement journey was suddenly cut short when she died shortly after her retirement began. My parents' retirement journeys demonstrate how you never know how your retirement will play out, which is why

4. "Facts & Figures," RAGBRAI, 2025, https://ragbrai.com/facts-and-figures/

planning as early as possible is crucial. The sooner you start planning, the more time you have to save and position yourself for a sustainable and enjoyable retirement.

I have found that we all need to talk about these things. In my retirement planning seminars, I typically say: "Let's talk about something that no one wants to talk about. We frequently don't want to talk about things that are different or difficult."

Before I became a financial advisor, I would volunteer helping people in my church with their personal finances. What I saw during that experience was that without some advanced planning, there was only so much I could do to help. When I expressed my frustration to my pastor, he suggested that I start giving seminars designed to help pre-retirees plan better for their future. I did, and that started me out on the career that I now have today, which I have enjoyed for more than 20 years.

CREATING DAILY ROUTINES

For the journey to be as smooth as possible, planning and foresight are incredibly important. To transition from the working life that makes retirement possible into actually retiring, the first thing I ask clients to consider is what they want their days and weeks to look like.

While the rhythm of work dictated what was possible in the rest of the day's schedule, and the whole week at large, there are now infinite possibilities for you to shape your schedule. And a lot of these decisions come back to the passions of each retiree—which means you need to determine how you will shape your days.

If you're like many of my clients, you worked a traditional 8 or 9 a.m. to 5 p.m. job. Then, either before or after work or on the weekends, you had to fit in your other activities. Suddenly, you've got a big canvas of time to work with, and you don't want to waste an opportunity you've worked so hard to enjoy.

Some people are so settled in their work routines that they will continue to get up at the same time that they did when they worked; others enjoy sleeping later. Consider how you will structure your days—what activities appeal to you and how might you integrate them into your day?

There's a saying that I know many of my married clients identify with in retirement: for better, for worse, in sickness and health, but not for lunch! Many women who have been homemakers or who have retired before their husbands have routines set up that they aren't necessarily eager to have disrupted by the presence of a spouse with too much time on their hands. Some wives are very self-sufficient because their spouses traveled a great deal for work and weren't home that often during the week. This can create a challenge in retirement, and we help our clients deal with that. It's not uncommon to see clients who would roll their eyes at their husbands when they discussed being home after a busy career spent traveling.

Discussing these issues with each other and talking about how your schedules will mesh before you retire is ideal, because you don't want annoyance to disrupt a time in your life that you've waited so long to enjoy.

A PLACE TO CALL HOME

When considering retirement, you should consider all of the big factors in life and leave no stone unturned. Deciding where to live during retirement is one thing that a lot of pre-retirees have already considered when we begin to discuss options, and this makes it a natural starting point from where the other decisions flow.

The family home is the place where a lot of clients still reside when beginning to seriously plan for retirement. A lot of the time this means that the kids are out of the house, and what's left may be much bigger and more expensive to maintain than would be optimal going into a retirement where the plan is to maximize quality of life and enjoyment. This can be a difficult conversation. The family home is a source of pride and a wellspring of memory that is very difficult to let go of. Some people identify keeping the family home as their number one priority, and if that's you then we can figure it out.

However, to start out we like to keep all options on the table. Owning a home is expensive under the best of circumstances. The first consideration is whether the house is owned outright or on a mortgage. And in the planning phase, there is often still time for adjustment. If the main goal is to keep the house, then we make plans to pay down the debt in advance of retirement, make any big repairs or renovations while there is still cash flow from work, and be sure to set aside savings to pay for the unexpected expenses that always end up cropping up for homeowners.

If paying off your mortgage and putting aside funds for future repairs is not possible, that's where we can circle back to conversations about other sources of income in retirement—consulting, income from a new business, rental property income and other opportunities to resolve cash flow in the face of the challenges of home ownership. Many pre-retirees with children have the greatest desire to leave the family home to the children, as their legacy. This is admirable, and we can help you get there.

But sometimes life throws you a curveball, and the value of the house can be the lever to pull and help make other dreams come true. Some parents dream for decades of leaving behind the family house, but once they become grandparents, they realize that their priority is actually to be as close to their grandchildren as possible, and oftentimes this means moving. This can be a blessing in disguise, as the value of many of these family houses exceeds the cost of a new, smaller home. Others have planned to downsize all along. Either way, there are a handful of important considerations that we can help navigate.

No matter the circumstances, however, selling a home often involves coming to grips with some hard truths. Many pre-retirees bought their home a couple decades ago, and although the economic conditions of an area are largely outside of any one individual's influence, they have an effect on the value of the home during this time.

When you're selling the family home, there are several things to consider outside of the sale itself. The first is obvious: where will you move to? For some the choice to downsize and move comes from the same familial motivations as keeping the home, so that can mean moving closer to relatives, whether that be children, grandchildren, siblings, or other relatives. One issue to consider is that as of the writing of this book in 2025 there was a shortage of one-story and other types of homes that would be suitable if you're thinking of aging in place, which can make it difficult to find a place to move into.[5]

And make no mistake, long-term health is a serious consideration when making these decisions about whether to downsize or not. There are a variety of options when it comes to considering long-term health, and knowing all of the possibilities can help make all of the other decisions more clear-cut. Many pre-retirees consider selling their home and moving into continuing care retirement communities. These are residential, planned communities that offer a range of living arrangements. Some retirees move out of a house into a retirement community where they still live independently in a house, while others may move into a condominium or apartment, and others still into a shared building where skilled nursing is readily available at all hours.

Thinking about giving up a degree of independence can be a bitter pill to swallow. However, it is important to be realistic. If "aging in place" is the most important priority for you, meaning you desire to stay in your family home for the rest of your life, there are important considerations that can be expected and accounted for. Without proper planning, however, these unexpected changes can hamstring an otherwise comfortable retirement. My own dad made the decision to retire and stay home, and we supported him, but had to make certain adjustments to the house. Many homes that have been in possession of one family for a long time will not have all the modern renovations that make living in old age comfortable. To account for Dad's decision, we had to spend a good amount of money to renovate the bathrooms and make them safe for his level of mobility.

---

5. "Aging in Place or Stuck in Place?" The New York Times, April 20, 2024, https:// www.nytimes.com/2024/04/20/health/seniors-home-equity-mortgages.html

We can't have a conversation about where to live in retirement without considering a consequential decision that many of my clients wrestle with: whether to pay off their mortgage before they retire. Whether you should pay off your house is a decision you should approach thoughtfully—especially if you plan on using retirement funds to make the payoff.

My advice is not to automatically use retirement funds—especially funds in tax-deferred traditional accounts such as 401(k)s or IRAs—to pay off your mortgage, unless you've carefully evaluated the following four factors:

1. **Tax consequences:** Withdrawals from traditional retirement accounts are taxable income. If, for example, you decide to withdraw $100,000 from your tax-deferred retirement account to pay off your mortgage, you could be pushed into a higher tax bracket. The consequences of being in a higher tax bracket, even for one year, could include significantly higher taxes in addition to the taxes you will owe on that withdrawal. The additional taxes could outweigh any interest you'd save.
2. **Cash flow needs in retirement:** If your mortgage payment is manageable and your investments are earning more in interest, and your dividends or capital appreciation is more than your mortgage interest rate, you might be better off keeping your mortgage and maintaining your liquidity.
3. **Mortgage rate vs. investment return:** If your mortgage rate is low, such as 3 to 5%, and your investments are earning more, you may be better off keeping the loan. On the other hand, if peace of mind or a high rate matters more to you, paying off the loan could make sense.
4. **Emotional and psychological factors:** If you prioritize peace of mind and reduced monthly expenses, paying off your mortgage might make sense. If, however, you value flexibility

and liquidity over peace of mind and reduced expenses, it could make more sense to continue to pay your mortgage.

PHASES OF RETIREMENT

Decisions about how to spend your time in retirement and where to live are not distinct choices that exist in isolation. They are part of a larger trajectory that will comprise the—ideally many—years of retirement for each individual or couple. One way to think about this is as a set of plans for different parts of retirement: the Go-Go Years, the Slow-Go Years, and the No-Go Years.[6]

Dividing retirement into these three phases shows how much retirement is a journey—not just a single destination. We need to think about all the plans we need to put into place to help ensure your retirement journey is sustainable and enjoyable. There are many parts of your retirement journey that will evolve over time. Perhaps you want to travel, to fulfill all your bucket wishes from when you were working. But there will come a time when you may get tired of travel and want to be home more. I've seen that while every retirement journey is unique, there are some common themes that are fairly universal in retirement, as noted in the phases Go-Go, Slow-Go and No-Go.

6. "Three Phases of Retirement: How Your Spending Changes," Prana Wealth Management, 2025, https://www.pranawealth.com/three-phases-of-retirement-how-your-spending-changes/#

Go-Go Years: The Go-Go Years are the early years of retirement, which are usually the mid-60s to mid-70s. During this time, we like to plan for the majority of taxing activities: travel, opening a business, completing home renovations—all those activities that are potentially taxing on the body and the bank account. We plan for a higher level of spending during these years to help ensure it's then possible to live the rest of retirement comfortably and without regrets or wishes to have done something differently.

The Go-Go Years tend to be the healthiest years of retirement and the time when you want to check items off your bucket list—the activities that you wanted to do when you were working but didn't have the time to do. During these years, you're likely spending time traveling either on your own or with friends in a similar stage of life. You may enjoy an active lifestyle, including working out at the gym, participating in recreational sports, golfing, fitness classes, biking and more.

The Slow-Go Years: The middle years of retirement, the Slow-Go Years, in line with the previous entry, comprise the next decade or so, the mid-70s to mid-80s. During these years it will be common practice to slow things down, to still make good the promises of retirement regarding fulfilling dreams, but to have more of an eye on the happiness that can be found and achieved by staying closer to home. During these years you may experience additional health concerns, so having a good foundation of community and trusted care providers becomes more important here.

Typically, retirees in this phase have more medical concerns, and may be dealing with mobility issues. It isn't as easy to bounce back from, say, a trans-Atlantic flight as it used to be, so if you're traveling, it may be domestically rather than internationally. You may enjoy the slower pace that this time of life brings, enjoying nearby friends, restaurants and social activities. Spending tends to be the lowest in this phase of retirement.

You may find it difficult to accept some of the changes that come with the Slow-Go Years. In our practice, we meet a lot of people who do. Take this fictional example: consider someone whose mother was quite resistant to the modifications necessary for her to stay in her home. When grab bars were installed in her bathroom, she related to the technician installing them that she used the towel rack to steady herself and didn't need grab bars. When the technician replied that towel racks were there to hold up towels, not people, her mother stuck her tongue out at his back.

I've seen many clients who persist in doing all their own yard work—or even work on a farm—when that work is becoming too taxing from a physical standpoint. Overtaxing yourself can set the stage for an accident that may incapacitate you, even if that is only for a short period of time. I've asked clients if it really is worth breaking a hip rather than getting the help needed for lawn care or moving into a condo where yard work is included in the condo fee.

No-Go Years: The No-Go Years represent the final years of retirement, and generally start in the early or mid-80s. Even retirees who have been generally healthy may begin to encounter health problems at this stage. A decline in health is inevitable for most retirees, but carefully managed and planned for can still be a rewarding life on its own terms. This stage of retirement can bring sadness and grief with the loss of friends, relatives and even a spouse. Expenses tend to increase as healthcare needs rise and require more spending.

SPECIAL CONSIDERATIONS FOR BUSINESS OWNERS

As a business owner, you may be so consumed with running your business that you haven't given much thought to what your retirement journey might look like. But this is something that you need to put some effort into envisioning, so you can look forward to this inevitable step that we all need to take at some point. I can empathize, because I'm a business owner—it's easy to get so wrapped up in serving your clients and making their lives better that you neglect yourself.

It might help to think about your retirement and exit from your business as a package deal. If you're like me, you love your business, but you don't necessarily want to be running as hard as you are now for the rest of your life. In fact, you will want to—or need to—slow down at some point. Better that any slow down or exit come from you voluntarily than by necessity due to a health condition or inability to keep up.

Proactively engaging in planning for your next stage of life gives you more control over how and when you move on, rather than someone else or something else. Think about what you've wanted to do, but postponed due to your need to work on your business. Perhaps you've always wanted to go on a fishing trip to Alaska, a premier destination for fisherman, but you've never had the time to make it worthwhile. Or maybe you've got a 1968 Ford Mustang GT 390 sitting in your garage, ready for tinkering and a new engine, but you never had time to get to it. You could be one of those people who always has a craft project going but never have time to finish any of them. Or maybe you are itching to make a baby quilt for your new grandbaby, but your sewing machine has been gathering dust for the last decade.

Consider what you've wanted to spend time on but haven't been able to and how you might spend your days without the all-consuming work of your business. There's no doubt that retirement is a big change from the active life of a business owner, but the good news is that you may be able to stay involved in your business at a certain level after a sale. Perhaps you can stay on for a year or two as a part-time consultant or fill some other role to transition out.

CONSIDERATIONS FOR INDEPENDENT WOMEN

If you're a never-married, divorced or widowed woman, your retirement journey begins in your imagination. Without a spouse or partner to consult, you have the freedom to decide exactly how you want your retirement to look. That starts with considering how you want your days to look—considering what activities and relation-ships you will lean on to organize your days. We deal with this type of client also.

Of course, single men have to grapple with similar challenges; in our practice, we tend to see more single women, which is why I wanted to include information like this in the book. Take this as an example: Sally is politically active, sending out get-out-the-vote postcards to encourage people to exercise their right to vote and informing them about voter registration options if they aren't registered. She also helps take care of her 97-year-old father, takes ukulele lessons and knits.

You also want to look at the big picture. Will you stay in your current home or downsize? Do you want to stay where you live now, or move to a warmer climate? For many independent women, travel plays an important role in their retirement. I know of several independent women who travel together regularly. Another one gets together yearly for a week with her college friends—they decide on a different destination every year. Many travel opportunities exist for solo travelers to travel with other single people and explore a variety of domestic and international destinations.

Understanding the various stages of retirement and how they are likely to unfold is an important consideration for independent women. There will likely come a point at which you need more care than you could receive in your own home or apartment. You may want to consider a continuing care community, where you could live independently and then move to higher levels of care such as assisted living when you can't live independently anymore.

UP NEXT

In Chapter 2, you'll learn how to evaluate your retirement readiness. Once you know how you want to spend your retirement, it's time to analyze your resources to see how they stack up to your ideal retirement journey.

2

EVALUATING YOUR RETIREMENT READINESS

When you consider retirement, you may experience conflicting emotions: excitement about entering a new phase in your life mixed with apprehension about what that new phase may bring. Retirement is a big step as you enter into a completely new reality. That reality involves stopping working, an activity that you've likely engaged in since your teens or early 20s.

Work isn't just your identity—it's also how you pay your bills. When you retire, you need to find a new focus not just for how you spend your time, but also how you generate income. You may love your work, or you may be tired of working. There's usually a range of emotions when retirement begins to transform from an idea into a reality.

What I find is that many of my clients are initially apprehensive about retirement, but when they find that they can actually afford to retire, their hesitation is replaced by relief. If you're like my clients, you've been saving for a long time—your entire career. You've sacrificed enjoyment and fun in the present for the future. The question at this point in your career is whether you are ready to take the next step—are you prepared for a comfortable, worry-free retirement?

That's why I'm addressing retirement readiness in this second chapter. You can't plan for retirement if you don't know whether you are ready or not. A first step in assessing your retirement readiness involves ensuring that you have sufficient funds to last throughout a retirement. At this point, I ask my clients: "Are you ready to be unemployed for the next 25 to 30 years?" I pose the question provocatively on purpose, because most pre-retirees don't frame retirement in that way, but that is exactly what a work-free retirement involves.

Other topics I will cover in this chapter involve taxes, health insurance, health, Social Security, the optimal age to retire, debt, legacies and a variety of retirement risks. Retirement is a journey, not a destination and it takes planning to get there, and to remain there in a comfortable and worry-free fashion.

ENOUGH MONEY FOR A LONG RETIREMENT

Life expectancy is one of the major wild cards in retirement. The Social Security Life Expectancy Calculator predicts that a 65-year-old woman born on March 1, 1960, is likely to live until an average age of 86.9.[1] A man, born on the same day, who is also 65, is likely to live until 84.3.[2] You need to plan for a retirement that could last 25 to 30 years, which is why you must have enough financial resources to ensure that you won't run out of money at the worst possible time—in extreme old age.

When I assess retirement readiness from the financial point of view, I analyze sources of savings and income, any expressed needs or wishes to help and support others, the potential difficulty of unretiring and the ability to live your preferred lifestyle. For most of my clients, savings come in the form of company-sponsored retirement plans such as 401(k)s or 403(b)s. Others have savings in the form of pensions from either the government or a private company. Some have both—retirement savings and a pension.

---

1. "Retirement & Survivors Benefits: Life Expectancy Calculator," US Social Security Administration, March 2, 2025, https://www.ssa.gov/cgi-bin/longevity.cgi

2. "Retirement & Survivors Benefits: Life Expectancy Calculator," US Social Security Administration, March 2, 2025, https://www.ssa.gov/cgi-bin/longevity.cgi

In these uncertain times, many pre-retirees and retirees are providing financial support to their children and even their grandchildren. In fact, nearly half of U.S. parents asked in a Savings.com survey reported providing some type of financial support to their adult children in 2023.[3] The average amount of support provided to adult children was $1,384 monthly, more than twice that of what those surveyed were contributing to their retirement accounts.[4] Some of my clients find themselves in this situation, where their support for their adult children may compromise their ability to retire as soon as they would like.

Another factor in the financial retirement readiness calculation comes in the form of how difficult it is to un-retire and go back to work should you find yourself in a situation where you don't have enough income. No one really wants to unretire and become a greeter at Wal-Mart. And the fact is, job security is uncertain. Layoffs in large companies and the government show that many people who aren't ready to retire are propelled in that direction by a job loss later in life.

Many pre-retirees plan to work longer than they actually do work. That means they often retire sooner than they believe they will, which can have significant financial repercussions. The average pre-retiree plans to retire at age 67, but typically ends up retiring at age 62, a five-year difference.[5] Corporate layoffs, declining health and lack of workplace satisfaction are the most frequent triggers of an expectedly early retirement.[6]

---

3. "Nearly 50% of US parents financially supporting adult children, study finds," The Guardian, March 12, 2024, https://www.theguardian.com/us-news/2024/mar/12/parents-adult-children-financial-support

4. "Nearly 50% of US parents financially supporting adult children, study finds," The Guardian, March 12, 2024, https://www.theguardian.com/us-news/2024/mar/12/parents-adult-children-financial-support

5. "Think you'll work past 70? Good luck. Why most of us retire earlier," USA Today, Jan. 30, 2024, https://www.usatoday.com/story/money/2024/01/24/most-americans-retire-earlier-than-expected-over-their-health-layoffs/72312011007/

6. "Think you'll work past 70? Good luck. Why most of us retire earlier," USA Today, Jan. 30, 2024, https://www.usatoday.com/story/money/2024/01/24/most-americans-retire-earlier-than-expected-over-their-health-layoffs/72312011007/

One example I've seen within my clientele are corporate buyouts. I've seen these situations at companies like Duke Energy or Michelin in the Greenville, South Carolina area where I have my financial advisory practice. Companies like these will periodically offer severance packages to their employees. Usually, employees hear rumors that a cutback is planned due to some type of internal or external change. Perhaps there has been a management change, or perhaps economic circumstances are volatile. Whatever the reason, rumors usually start that a layoff is coming, targeting certain departments.

For employees who have worked at companies like these for many decades—frequently their entire careers—these rumors are concerning because they could get laid off without any extra pay or benefits. My clients who had planned to work another two, three or five years can get especially concerned. That's when they come into the office for a retirement readiness analysis. They ask me, "What am I going to do? Am I actually ready for retirement?" If a severance package is offered, they wonder if they should take it, or risk being laid off without it.

I will talk to these clients or potential clients and go over their situation. Frequently, I meet with one-income households where the wife is a homemaker or households where the man is the primary breadwinner, and the wife works part time. I see a lot of nervousness because they worry about whether they will have enough income and also, what they will do about health insurance if they have to retire before age 65.

In most cases, we are able to come up with strategies, many of which are included in this book, so that they can take the severance package and have enough income to make it through retirement. There is usually a way to handle the health insurance through the federal health insurance exchange, through a COBRA policy from the employer, or perhaps they get some health benefits as part of the severance package. When it works out, they are so excited and so relieved. In many cases, the severance packages offer a year at their current salary along with health insurance benefits, so they can get a year of potential growth out of their investments before they need to depend on them for retirement income.

I've personally experienced a similar situation where a forced retirement left my Dad unable to send me to college. As the youngest of 13 children, I was graduating from high school when my Dad had to retire. As much as he wanted to help pay for my college, like he had with a number of my siblings, he did not have the resources to do that because my parents were trying to figure out how they were going to get through their retirement. Because of this forced retirement, I had to make my own way and figure out how to pay for college. I actually did get to college, but then in my sophomore year, my Dad got sick, so I had to come home and help out. I transferred to a local college.

Like many in their generation, my parents didn't have a retirement plan. They essentially had a choice between spending their money to send their last child—me—to college or being able to retire. I remember how hurt my Dad was that he could not help me. As a result of this situation, my experience was significantly different from that of my sister, who is next to me in age, because my parents were able to assist with her college expenses. I worked hard to find the money to get through college through a combination of scholarships, student loans, work-study programs and more. When I came home to help my family after my Dad got sick, I worked full-time and went to school.

I learned how big an impact retirement can have because of this situation. My Dad's forced retirement affected not just my Dad, but me and the rest of my family—it trickled down to my journey. Looking back, I can see how my passion to help people ensure their own retirement readiness was influenced by what my Dad and my family went through. That's why I get so much satisfaction out of helping others prepare for a sustainable retirement. I learned how important it is to start thinking about retirement earlier than you think you should. If you wait, it isn't too late, but at that point you may have fewer options.

Regardless of whether you take a severance package, get laid off or work until you are ready to leave your job, you want a comfortable, worry-free retirement. As I related in Chapter 1, focusing on your top priorities in retirement is crucial, but that means something different to each pre-retiree. For some, that might involve travel. For others, starting a new business is important after decades spent working for others. You may want to move to live near your children and grandchildren and help with their education. Our job together is to help ensure that you have the financial wherewithal to pursue those goals and remain in a sustainable financial place.

HOW MUCH OF YOUR RETIREMENT INCOME DO YOU GET TO KEEP?

Having enough money to retire comfortably isn't as important as being able to keep enough income to maintain your desired lifestyle. Taxes can have a big impact on your retirement income in ways that you might not expect.

Many pre-retirees receive most of their retirement income from taxable sources such as pensions, Social Security and traditional IRA and 401(k) accounts. Essentially, you need to discount the amount of money you have in those accounts by the taxes that may be due when you either receive Social Security or a pension—or both—or take distributions from your pre-tax retirement accounts. Depending on your income, your Social Security could be taxed up to 50 to 85% of your benefit.[7] Pension income and distributions from pre-tax retirement accounts are taxed at ordinary income rates.[8,9]

Taxes can have other unanticipated impacts on your income and expenses, especially once you become eligible for Medicare. Premiums for Medicare Part B, which covers services from doctors, outpatient

7. "Social Security Benefit Taxation Highlights," Sept. 23, 2024, https://crsreports.con gress.gov/product/pdf/IF/IF11397/3

8. "Pensions and Annuity Withholding," U.S. Internal Revenue Service, Oct. 30, 2024, https://www.irs.gov/individuals/international-taxpayers/pensions-and-annuity-with holding

9. "IRAs FAQs—Distributions (withdrawals)," July 30, 2024, https://www.irs.gov/retirement-plans/retirement-plans-faqs-regarding-iras-distributions-withdrawals#

hospital services, home health services and more, are income-based.[10] That means if your modified adjusted gross income exceeds a certain amount, you will pay higher Medicare premiums.[11] For example, if you are married, filing jointly, and have modified adjusted gross income greater than or equal to $212,000 and less than or equal to $266,000, your Medicare Part B premium would be $259 a month, an increase of $74 over the basic premium of $185 a month—each.[12] That may not happen immediately when you retire, depending on how old you are when you retire, but it could happen over time.

However, over time, you will claim Social Security at some point on or before your 70th birthday, which could translate into taxable income.[13] When you turn 73, you must begin taking Required Minimum Distributions (RMDs), assuming you have savings in tax-deferred retirement accounts.[14] My point is that while you may think that you will pay less in taxes in retirement, that may not be the case, which means part of assessing your retirement readiness involves analyzing your tax situation.

The following graphic illustrates what possible income, expenses and net income could look like in retirement. As always, each person's situation is unique to them.

---

10. "2025 Medicare Parts A & B Premiums and Deductibles," U.S. Centers for Medicaid and Medicare, Nov. 8, 2024, https://www.cms.gov/newsroom/fact-sheets/2025-medicare-parts-b-premiums-and-deductibles

11. "2025 Medicare Parts A & B Premiums and Deductibles," U.S. Centers for Medicaid and Medicare, Nov. 8, 2024, https://www.cms.gov/newsroom/fact-sheets/2025-medicare-parts-b-premiums-and-deductibles

12. "2025 Medicare Parts A & B Premiums and Deductibles," U.S. Centers for Medicaid and Medicare, Nov. 8, 2024, https://www.cms.gov/newsroom/fact-sheets/2025-medicare-parts-b-premiums-and-deductibles

13. "Social Security Benefit Taxation Highlights," Sept. 23, 2024, https://crsreports.con gress.gov/product/pdf/IF/IF11397/3

14. "IRAs FAQs—Distributions (withdrawals)," July 30, 2024, https://www.irs.gov/retirement-plans/retirement-plans-faqs-regarding-iras-distributions-withdrawals#

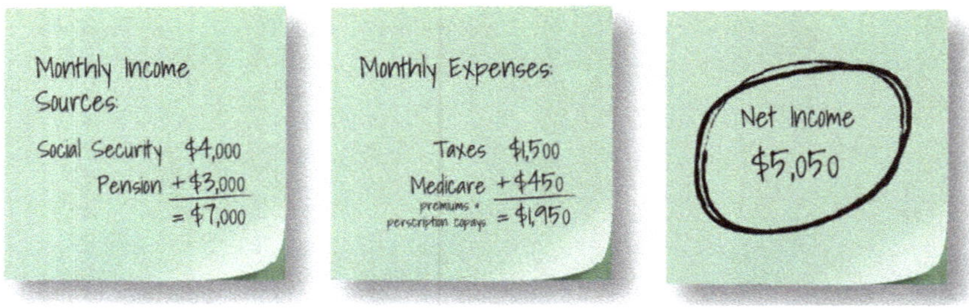

Hypothetical example shown for illustrative purposes only, actual figures will vary.

HEALTH INSURANCE AND HEALTH

If you're thinking about retiring before you are eligible to claim Medicare at age 65, you need to plan for healthcare coverage to fill in the gap until you are eligible. Many of my clients who are in this situation can find health insurance coverage on the U.S. government health insurance marketplace, where you can find a variety of health insurance options and sign up for coverage.

At age 65, claiming Medicare isn't just one decision. You also have to decide whether to sign up for traditional Medicare or a Medicare Advantage Plan, a type of bundled care offered through private insurers where you will receive all your healthcare through a specific network of healthcare providers and hospitals that includes Medicare Part A, Part B and often Part D.[15]

If you are younger than age 65, you need to decide what type of healthcare exchange plan to get, which usually depends on the benefits that you want and the premiums, deductibles and copays necessary to pay for those services.

Health insurance, of course, is of prime importance because as you age, more health issues are likely to arise. The National Council

---

15. "Understanding Medicare Advantage Plans," U.S. Centers for Medicare and Medicaid, March 3, 2025, https://www.medicare.gov/publications/12026-understanding-medicare-advantage-plans.pdf

on Aging notes that older Americans are disproportionately affected by chronic diseases like diabetes, heart disease and arthritis as nearly 95% of those age 65 and older have one or more of those conditions, while 80% have two or more.[16] These facts underline the importance of carefully choosing the Medicare plan or healthcare exchange plan that is right for you.

WHEN TO CLAIM SOCIAL SECURITY

You have an eight-year window to claim, optimize and maximize Social Security—from ages 62 to 70. The size of your monthly benefits depends on how much you earned during your career, how many years you worked and when you claim.

If you were born in 1960 or later, which is the case for most pre-retirees today, your full retirement age is 67. If you claim earlier than age 67, you will receive a lower benefit, depending on how much earlier you claim benefits.[17] For example, if you claim benefits at age 62, your monthly benefit will be 30% less than if you waited until age 67.[18] If your monthly benefit at full retirement age was $2,000, then your benefit at age 62 would be $1,400.

If you claim later than age 67, your benefit will be higher than your full retirement benefit. When you wait to claim your benefit, you receive an additional 8% of your benefit amount for each year you wait through age 70.[19] That means if you had the same $2,000 a monthly benefit at age 67, waiting to claim until age 70 would increase your benefit by 24% to $2,480 a month.

---

16. "Get the Facts on Healthy Aging," National Council on Aging," Aug. 16, 2024, https://www.ncoa.org/article/get-the-facts-on-healthy-aging/

17. "Starting Your Retirement Benefits Early," U.S. Social Security Administration, March 4, 2025, https://www.ssa.gov/benefits/retirement/planner/agereduction.html

18. "Starting Your Retirement Benefits Early," U.S. Social Security Administration, March 4, 2025, https://www.ssa.gov/benefits/retirement/planner/agereduction.html

19. "Delayed Retirement Credits," U.S. Social Security Administration, March 4, 2025, https://www.ssa.gov/benefits/retirement/planner/delayret.html

Social Security claiming isn't just about your own benefit—if you are married, you need to coordinate claiming with your spouse to achieve the best possible outcome. In cases where the male spouse is the main breadwinner and is at least several years older than his wife, the decision about when to claim is quite nuanced. This is because you don't want to leave your spouse in need of income after you pass away. Women typically live longer than men, and if you are already older than your wife, it is likely that she will outlive you by a number of years. In these situations, I will work closely with you to craft a maximizing Social Security claiming strategy—along with an entire retirement income plan—to help ensure that your wife is taken care of after you pass away. I obtained the National Social Security Advisor designation to acquire the knowledge of the workings of Social Security I needed to help my clients understand their claiming options better.

You also need to consider how best to coordinate all your income sources to provide the most optimal income stream to support achieving your ideal retirement lifestyle. Deciding when to claim Social Security and proactively engaging in a coordinated benefit strategy will help you determine when you're ready to retire.

OPTIMAL AGE TO RETIRE

There is no optimal age to retire—the ideal age to retire is when you are ready from both an ideal retirement journey and readiness point of view. For some of my clients, that happens earlier, while others wait until they are more prepared. What I find frequently is that when clients understand that they possess the financial resources to embark on their ideal retirement journey, they find they want to retire more quickly than they had previously thought.

There's an obvious tension built into the decision about when to retire. If you retire early, you might be concerned about whether you will outlive your savings. If you wait to retire until later, you might be concerned about your health declining and being unable to enjoy travel, spending time with your family and other activities that you've postponed during your working years.

I work with my clients to help them find the sweet spot in their life where they can have enough money to enjoy retirement while they are still healthy and able to enjoy checking items off on their bucket list.

LEAVING A LEGACY

Along with a comfortable retirement, leaving a legacy for future generations and favorite causes is high on my clients' lists of retirement wishes. For some, that wish involves passing wealth to future generations. For others, they want to build a family business in retirement that can support their families now and in the future. Still others seek to make an impact on the wider world through charitable giving to favorite causes.

Legacy planning is an important part of evaluating your retirement readiness. You don't want your generosity to others to crimp your lifestyle or dreams for your ideal retirement. Assessing where you are, how much you want to give and in what ways you will ultimately give can be integrated into your overall retirement plan.

Some of my clients actively integrate their legacy planning into their life by starting a business with their family members with an eye towards building that business over time so it can support children and even grandchildren in the future. Others might set aside a certain amount of money to fund college savings accounts for their grandchildren or help pay for day care. Some add this to their estate plan by working with me and an estate planning attorney to leave money to their families after they pass away.

RETIREMENT RISK FACTORS

A final consideration in evaluating your retirement readiness is the risk factors common to retirement. The most common risk factors are longevity, death of a spouse, market volatility, rising interest rates, climate change, and long-term care. While there are other risks, these are the ones that we believe most impact your retirement readiness.

Longevity Risk: Longevity risk is the risk that you will live longer than you expect.[20] As I've mentioned, the lifespans of affluent Americans are increasing, which means that many pre-retirees could live into their mid-to-late 80s or even into their 90s. If you retire at age 65, a long lifespan means essentially being unemployed for at least 20 years, if not longer. That means you need to rely on your financial resources to support you during that entire lifespan, especially when you become older and frailer.

As I've explained, elderly people typically have more health problems than younger people. In my experience, healthcare expenses tend to increase in later retirement, as retirees experience problems with mobility, chronic illnesses and other illnesses like cancer, which can necessitate long-term care. Fidelity Benefits Consulting reported that retirees spend on healthcare in three different ways during retirement:[21]

- 47% of spending goes for co-pays, deductibles and co-insurance for doctor and hospital visits.
- 44% of spending goes toward Medicare Part B and Part D premiums, doctor's appointments and hospital visits.
- 9% of spending goes toward medications, including generics, branded drugs and specialty drugs.

The longer you live, the longer you will be paying healthcare costs. The Fidelity Retiree Health Care Cost Estimate for 2025 projects that the average 65-year-old retiring in 2024 will spend $172,500 on healthcare in retirement.[22] In contrast, Americans

20. How to Manage Longevity Risk in Retirement," Kiplinger.com, Dec .10, 2024, https://www.kiplinger.com/retirement/retirement-planning/how-to-manage-longevity-risk-in-retirement

21. "Where does retiree health care money go? Fidelity, 2024, https://institutional. fidelity.com/advisors/insights/spotlights/retirement-income-planning/retirement-planning-health-care-costs

22. "Fidelity Investments Releases 2025 Retiree Health Care Cost Estimate, A Timely Reminder for All Generations to Begin Planning," Fidelity, Jul. 30, 2025: https://news room.fidelity.com/pressreleases/fidelity-investments--releases-2025-retiree-health-care-cost-estimate--a-timely-reminder-for-all-gen/s/3c62e988-12e2-4dc8-afb4-f44b06c6d52e.

surveyed by Fidelity expect to spend $75,000 on healthcare expenses in retirement.[23]

As those costs increase, you need to make sure you are prepared. Healthcare costs, which are always unpredictable, can be even more unpredictable in retirement. Working with an experienced financial advisor can help you create a retirement income plan that will cover the likely eventuality of higher healthcare costs in retirement.

Death of a Spouse Risk: No one likes to think about losing their spouse—it can be one of the most difficult parts of aging. We all hope that we will have a long life with our spouse, but it doesn't always work out that way. I've heard too many stories of couples who waited to retire only to experience a short time together before one of them passed much earlier than expected. Consider the tragic example of a friend of a friend who was traveling with her husband in their motor home when he accidentally fell, experienced a head injury and died shortly thereafter. Fictional in this case, but it happens. There are also many other cases of spouses being diagnosed with cancer or other terminal illnesses at an early stage in retirement. Losing a spouse is emotionally devastating and can also be financially devastating. Frequently, the burden of financial challenges in retirement falls on women.

Because women have longer lifespans and tend to be younger than their husbands, women tend to be widowed more frequently than men. More than three times as many widows were identified as widowers over age 60 in the 2020 U.S. Census.[24] In addition, because women are more likely than men to take time out of the workforce for caregiving and make less than men, women suffer from what is known as the

---

23. "Fidelity Health Solutions Thought Leadership Employer Health Benefits Blue-print" Fidelity, 2023, https://newsroom.fidelity.com/pressreleases/fidelity-investments--releases-2024-retiree-health-care-cost-estimate-as-americans-seek-clarity-arou/s/7322c c17-0b90-46c4-ba49-38d6e91c3961

24. "The impact of widowhood on the mental health of older adults and the buffering effect of social capital," Frontiers in Public Health, April 24, 2024, https://pmc.ncbi.nlm.nih.gov/articles/PMC11076834/#:~:text=According%20to%20data%20from%20the,measures%20and%20paths%20for%20improvement.

Retirement Income Gap.[25] Women receive an average of 24.7% less in Social Security benefits and have 38.7% less accumulated in retirement savings accounts.[26]

Another factor in death of a spouse risk that you might not be aware of is that when a spouse dies, only the larger of the two Social Security benefits is available to the surviving spouse. Let's say, for example Sue and Steve (imagined for this example) are a married couple in their 80s—Steve's Social Security benefit is $2,500 a month and Sue's is $1,500 a month. When Steve passes away, his Social Security benefit will transfer to Sue, because it is larger, and Sue's benefit will cease. Many couples depend on both their Social Security benefits for income in retirement, so losing one benefit can have a negative impact on financial status.

Market Risk: Market risk is the risk that the stock market volatility will negatively affect your retirement nest egg, leading to lower savings values in retirement and potentially lower income.[27] Market volatility is concerning enough when you are still working, but when you are in retirement and depend on your savings to last throughout your retirement, it can be especially difficult. Bear markets can wreak havoc on a retirement investment portfolio. While bear markets have historically ended and then turned into bull markets, there is no guarantee when this will happen or how low the markets might fall.[28]

Imagine finally retiring, only to have a bear market strike. This is the reality many retirees experienced during the financial crisis of 2007-09 and during the COVID bear market of March and April

---

25. "The Retirement Income Gap Leaves Women Aged 65+ at Higher Risk of Poverty Than Men," Institute for Women's Policy Research, May 2024, https://iwpr.org/wp-con tent/uploads/2024/05/IWPR-Retirement-Income-Gap-Quick-Figure-2024-1.pdf

26. "The Retirement Income Gap Leaves Women Aged 65+ at Higher Risk of Poverty Than Men," Institute for Women's Policy Research, May 2024, https://iwpr.org/wp-con tent/uploads/2024/05/IWPR-Retirement-Income-Gap-Quick-Figure-2024-1.pdf

27. "How to Prepare for the Risks to Your Retirement Savings," Thrivent, Jan. 10, 2025, https://www.thrivent.com/insights/retirement-planning/how-to-prepare-for-the-risks-to-your-retirement-savings

28. "What We've Learned from 150 Years of Stock Market Crashes," Morningstar, March 6, 2025, https://www.morningstar.com/economy/what-weve-learned-150-years-stock-market-crashes

2020.[29] There is a special name for this type of risk known as sequence of returns risk, which occurs when negative market returns occur at the beginning of your retirement, potentially permanently impairing the value of your retirement savings if you are taking regular withdrawals to fund your retirement.[30]

For these reasons, it is important to understand market and sequence of returns risk and to proactively develop a strategy to deal with these risks in retirement. When I create a retirement income plan with my clients, these risks are dealt with in the plan so that clients are positioned to help them weather market declines that can put their financial security at risk.

Interest Rate Risk: Like markets, interest rates vary—sometimes they are low, and other times they are high. When interest rates are low, they can make it difficult for retirees to earn a decent interest rate on their savings.[31] Rising interest rates negatively impact bond prices as the prices of existing bonds fall, which can affect retirees who have investments in bonds, bond funds and bond exchange-traded funds.[32]

From the mid-1980s through 2022, the U.S. experienced a period of very low interest rates. However, the U.S. Federal Reserve Board (the Fed) raised interest rates consistently during 2022 and 2023 and then began to cut rates again in 2024.[33] At the beginning of 2025, the Fed kept rates steady.[34] Because interest rate policies are constantly

---

29. "What We've Learned from 150 Years of Stock Market Crashes," Morningstar, March 6, 2025, https://www.morningstar.com/economy/what-weve-learned-150-years-stock-market-crashes

30. "Three Ways to Reduce Sequence of Returns Risk," Forbes.com, Sept. 25, 2024, https://www.forbes.com/councils/forbesfinancecouncil/2024/09/25/three-ways-to-reduce-sequence-of-return-risk/

31. "What Do Lower Interest Rates Mean for Retirees?" US News and World Report, Dec. 18, 2024, https://money.usnews.com/money/retirement/articles/what-do-lower-interest-rates-mean-for-retirees

32. "How Changing Interest Rates Impact the Bond Market," US Bank, Feb. 27, 2025, https://www.usbank.com/investing/financial-perspectives/market-news/interest-rates-affect-bonds.html

33. "Federal Reserve Calibrates Policy to Keep Inflation in Check," US Bank Wealth

34. "Federal Reserve Calibrates Policy to Keep Inflation in Check," US Bank Wealth Management, Jan. 31, 2025, https://www.usbank.com/investing/financial-perspectives/market-news/federal-reserve-tapering-asset-purchases.html

changing, individual retirees can find keeping up with the implications of interest rate changes challenging.

Like market risk, you'll want to understand how interest rates can affect your investment portfolio and how a retirement income plan can proactively deal with interest rate risk. I work with my clients to create a retirement income plan with diversified sources of income and a diversified investment portfolio to help mitigate the impact of interest rate risk on retirement.

Extreme Weather Risk: Severe and extreme weather events can devastate a retirement. Consider victims of the 2025 Los Angeles fires, where 11,200 homes and commercial buildings were destroyed in the Eaton and Palisades fires.[35] In North Carolina, approximately 73,700 homes were damaged during Hurricane Helene in October 2024.[36] Many victims of these natural disasters lacked sufficient insurance, which was potentially catastrophic.[37]

Losing your home in retirement—or any time—is immensely stressful, both emotionally and financially. Rebuilding may be too expensive, in which case you would need to find another place to live, which would involve a whole different set of costs regardless of whether you buy or rent. You may be left with a mortgage that you need to continue to pay without the ability to rebuild.

Extreme weather events can have other impacts on retirement, Management, Jan. 31, 2025, https://www.usbank.com/investing/financial-perspectives/market-news/federal-reserve-tapering-asset-purchases.html including causing health problems and increasing costs related to those events, such as insurance. A robust retirement

35. "New Analysis of LA Fires Reveals Property Damages Top $30 billion," Costar, Jan. 30, 2025, https://www.costar.com/article/1384517962/new-analysis-of-la-fires-reveals-property-damages-top-30-billion

36. "Hurricane Helene's Devastation Dominates 2024 Housing News in North Carolina," NCNewsline.com, Dec. 28, 2024, https://ncnewsline.com/2024/12/28/hurricane-helenes-devastation-dominates-2024-housing-news-in-north-carolina/

37. "Experts Warn that Victims of Major Disasters will Now Face New Obstacle to Recovery: 'Devastated,'" The Weather Channel, March 6, 2025, https://www.yahoo.com/news/experts-warn-victims-major-disasters-111545768.html

income plan will account for the potential risks that extreme weather events can create in retirement.

Long-Term Care Risk: Long-term care risk is the risk that you will need some kind of long-term care in retirement. Long-term care might include nursing home case, assisted living or home healthcare. Research from the Center for Retirement Research at Boston College estimated that approximately 25% of 65-year-olds will have severe long-term care needs, which involves nursing home care or daily needs for home healthcare.[38] Costs for these types of care can run between $61,000 a year for home care and $108,000 a year for nursing home care.[39]

Even moderate long-term care needs can cost tens of thousands of dollars a year. There's no predicting who will need care when planning for retirement, which means that it makes sense to plan for the worst-case scenario. Consider the example, again made up for this book to demonstrate a point, of a couple who owned a very successful restaurant that they worked in together. Over the course of owning this restaurant for 35 years, they scrimped and saved so their daughters could have the education that they never had and so that they could enjoy retirement. Just before they signed the papers to sell their restaurant, the husband had a stroke. In the operating room, the worse-case scenario happened, as the blood clot traveled to his brain, causing a permanent disability where he was not able to speak or take care of himself. This resulted in more than 20 years of expensive long-term care that has nearly drained their joint life savings.

As I tell my clients, failing to plan means planning to fail. You don't want to find yourself in a situation where you or your spouse needs some type of long-term care, and you don't know how you are going

38. "A Major Risk Facing Older Americans: The Need for Long-Term Care," The Center for Retirement Research, March 18, 2024, https://crr.bc.edu/a-major-risk-facing-older-americans-the-need-for-long-term-care/

39. "A Major Risk Facing Older Americans: The Need for Long-Term Care," The Center for Retirement Research, March 18, 2024, https://crr.bc.edu/a-major-risk-facing-older-americans-the-need-for-long-term-care/

to pay for it. That's why I work with my clients to assess what kinds of long-term care they might need and to proactively make a plan to help mitigate this retirement risk.

SPECIAL CONSIDERATIONS FOR BUSINESS OWNERS

As a business owner, you likely have a different perspective on retirement than those who are employed. Your business is something you have worked very hard on, and you may have a good amount of your retirement assets tied up in that business. But just like everyone else, you need to understand the state of your financial readiness. That includes considering the following questions:

- What are your retirement assets separate from your business?
- What amount do you expect to get from your business to support your retirement?
- Does your spouse have separate retirement assets from yours? If so, what are those assets?
- Do you have an exit plan for your business? (We will discuss this more in Chapter 3)

You'll also need to decide when you optimally want to retire, although if you are selling a business, there are many factors involved in a business sale that may not optimally line up with your ideal retirement date. Your ideal retirement date, retirement assets and other factors will inform when you want to claim Social Security.

Taxes can play a big factor in a business sale, because if you don't structure a sale carefully, you may have to pay a significant amount of taxes associated with the proceeds of the business. You also need to think about the amount of income you want to see monthly in retirement and what your expenses will be.

SPECIAL CONSIDERATIONS FOR INDEPENDENT WOMEN

Since you are independent, you have complete control over the financial decisions you make around your retirement. But if you're like my other independent women clients, you'll want to make sure that you are fully financially ready to retire when you are actually emotionally and mentally ready. Assessing your readiness involves dotting all the I's and crossing all the T's that I've mentioned above.

You'll likely want to make sure that you have more than enough saved to not only provide the monthly income you'll need to cover your expenses but also investments that will cover the other risks, such as long-term care and inflation risks. You'll want investments to also cover extra expenses, such as vacations, new cars when you need them, home renovations, etc.

For many independent women, it makes sense to wait to claim Social Security at age 70 to maximize the amount you can get in your monthly benefit. Since Social Security is indexed to inflation, your benefit will rise with inflation throughout your retirement. If you claim Social Security at age 62, which is the earliest possible age to claim, your benefit will be 70 percent of what you would receive if you waited until your full retirement age.[40] Full retirement age for anyone born in 1960 or later is 67.[41] If you wait until age 70 to claim, that means your benefit will be 124 percent of your benefit at full retirement age benefit.[42] If, for example, your full retirement age benefit was $3,000 a month, your benefit at age 62 would be $2,100 a month. If you waited to claim until age 70, your benefit would be $3,720.

---

40. "Guide on Taking Social Security: 62 vs. 67 vs. 70," CharlesSchwab.com, March 14, 2025, https://www.schwab.com/learn/story/guide-on-taking-social-security

41. "Guide on Taking Social Security: 62 vs. 67 vs. 70," CharlesSchwab.com, March 14, 2025, https://www.schwab.com/learn/story/guide-on-taking-social-security

42. "Guide on Taking Social Security: 62 vs. 67 vs. 70," CharlesSchwab.com, March 14, 2025, https://www.schwab.com/learn/story/guide-on-taking-social-security

A FINAL WORD

Now that you've gained some understanding of what it takes to be ready for retirement, we'll move on in Chapter 3 to aligning your retirement journey with your retirement readiness. This is the point at which a retirement income plan begins to take shape, taking into account your retirement readiness and your unique retirement journey.

3

ALIGNING YOUR RETIREMENT JOURNEY WITH YOUR RETIREMENT READINESS

Are you ready for retirement? The answer depends on what kind of readiness we're talking about. As a financial planner, I collaborate with my clients to help them prepare financially for retirement. But sometimes that isn't the most important type of readiness. In my more than 20 years working in retirement planning, I find that many of my clients struggle with the loss of identity and routine—that's what we call emotional readiness. A third type of readiness has to do with health and health insurance coverage, which involves expectations for your health in retirement and the best way to match your health needs with health insurance coverage.

Really, when we talk about readiness for retirement, we are talking about finding the right alignment between your journey, the challenges you will likely face, and the financial, emotional and health resources you have and will require to meet these challenges. A lot of this is hard to talk about—the prospect of losing your health and independence, for instance, is not something a lot of my clients want to hear about, because it's scary. This is precisely why it's important to have the hard conversations—to make sure you're ready when the unexpected happens, and in retirement, that is almost certain.

In this chapter I'll talk about three kinds of readiness for retirement: emotional, financial, and healthcare. I'll be outlining the common challenges I've observed my clients facing in retirement and describe some of the more common solutions.

THREE FACTORS OF RETIREMENT READINESS

EMOTIONAL READINESS

The emotional challenges associated with retirement shouldn't be underestimated. Some of the more common ones are dealing with a loss of identity that was previously associated with a career, deciding how to structure your time, adjusting to spending much more time with your partner and/or other family members than you used to, and replacing the relationships and activities that were associated with work.

Think about how you identify yourself to other people. "What do you do?" "I'm a teacher," or plumber, or whatever. Suddenly, in retirement, we don't necessarily do anything. Research has indicated that retirees who were strongly tied to their work role are more likely to experience diminished well-being, and this struggle with loss of identity is firmly linked to difficulties in establishing and maintaining financial goals.[1]

1. "How to Overcome Identity Loss in Retirement," Kiplinger, Jun. 4, 2024, https:// www.kiplinger.com/retirement/how-to-overcome-identity-loss-in-retirement

You can resolve this problem in a few ways. Some people continue to work in retirement, either in a diminished responsibility at their old place of business, or work in the same role as an independent contractor. Some even explore a new career. Keeping one foot in the workaday life can be advantageous to both your mind and your wallet—incidentally one study by the Employee Benefit Research Institute found that 88% of people working or planning to work during retirement said that the primary reason is that they enjoy work.[2]

If you don't want to work and don't need to, it's important to replace the activity you would see there. In this situation, there are many who find purpose in volunteering, doing charity work, and refocusing on their spiritual life as a member of a church, temple or mosque. Develop your hobbies—Bridge and Mah-Jong are stereotypical retired women activities, but that's because they do significant work relieving what would otherwise be empty hours. Similarly, stereotypical retirement male hobbies are fishing, hunting and golfing, or home renovations. Of course, a retired woman with enough talent and resources can certainly become a semi-pro golfer, just as a retired man can achieve success in the local semi-pro bridge tournaments.

Others will spend time traveling. Maybe you want to learn something new—it's likely that a university or community college in your area offers classes for retirees at a reduced or even nominal fee. Some recommit to their families—retirement is a chance to spend time with your grandchildren, after all. So, a lot of newly retired grandparents will spend significant amounts of time babysitting their grandchildren, which is of course rewarding but can be taken to extremes, as we'll see later.

One challenge of adjusting to retirement is so basic a lot of us don't even consider it. If you're married, chances are that you'll be spending a lot more "us time" than when you were working, and you need to be

---

2. Employee Benefit Research Institute, "2025 Retirement Confidence Survey Fact Sheet #2: Expectations About Retirement," Sep. 2025, https://www.ebri.org/docs/ default-source/rcs/2025-rcs/ rcs_25-fs-2.pdf?sfvrsn=f3e3042f_2.

able to cope with this. This is a big reason I see in my practice and why some of my clients keep working in their previous field—they literally can't hang around at home with their partner all day. Sometimes this is important and will help reduce strain on your marriage—a captain-of-industry type who retires and is used to bossing others around will start to micromanage his wife's activities, which isn't healthy for either partner.

Take this hypothetical example of a couple who could be my clients. They co-existed very compatibly because they each had their own activities. They would usually have meals together, but the husband, a retired professor, would golf, work out at the gym and read, while the wife, a retired elementary school teacher, would swim three days week and was also active in the retired county teachers' association, taught adult swimming lessons, and volunteered with local Friends of the Public Library.

Another thing to watch out for in retirement activities is the pursuit of pleasure. Say when you were working you didn't have enough time to pursue your hobby—let's say it's model trains. So, you start investing a comparable time that you had to work with the trains. Psychiatrists call what happens next "hedonic adaptation"—abundant access to the things we enjoy leads us to grow accustomed to them, and things we are accustomed to are less enjoyable. It's never good to throw all your expectations of enjoyment into one basket. This makes planning your days and weeks in retirement important. Having a routine increases our feelings of productivity and makes us less likely to struggle with loss of identity.[3]

One aspect of retired life that is enjoyable is that you can set your own schedule. If you are a night owl, you can stay up late and sleep late, whereas if you are a morning person, you can go to bed early and get up early. Once you've established those general parameters, you

---

3. "A Paradox in Retirement: You Need Structure in Your New Life," The David Miller Group at Morgan Stanley, May 3, 2024: https://advisor.morganstanley.com/david6. miller/documents/field/d/da/david-j--miller/A_Paradox_of_Retirement_WEB.pdf

can add various activities to your schedule. Perhaps you exercise or go for a walk after breakfast, then catch up on your email and bills. After lunch, you can engage in a hobby or volunteer activity and do some yard work. In the evenings, you can catch up on your favorite streaming shows and spend time with your spouse, friends and family. Exactly how you fill your schedule matters less than the fact that you have a schedule.

In the absence of a schedule, you can all too easily fall into aimlessness. That can involve lots of binge-watching streaming services, obsessive attention to the stock market and CNBC or binge shopping. Such habits don't promote mental, emotional or physical health, which is why creating a schedule before you retire is so important. Even if you eventually change your schedule, that's fine—intentionally deciding how you are going to spend your time is the point.

Overall, in retirement, the important thing is to develop a better idea—a better story—of who you are and what you do now that you're retired. Talking with a therapist can help with this process, and you're likely to also need family and community support to provide a sense of belonging and help you feel understood in the retirement transition.[4]

FINANCIAL READINESS

The financial challenge in retirement is simple: don't outlive your income. Though there are many other problems to deal with from a financial perspective, most of them can be reduced to income and spending.

Sometimes when we hit retirement, we find that our spending increases rather than reduces. Your home might need some remodeling, and you didn't have the time to give it attention while you were working full-time. Your car—or cars—may be outdated, in any case the car you have now is unlikely to last another 25 years, and you need something

4. "How to Overcome Identity Loss in Retirement," Kiplinger, Jun. 4, 2024, https:// www.kiplinger.com/retirement/how-to-overcome-identity-loss-in-retirement

that will last you through these years. Typically, my clients will buy a new or new-to-them car or cars in the year or two before they retire so they will have a vehicle that is relatively new and doesn't need repairs through the first part of retirement. Home remodeling may occur in the early years of retirement—this is something so common that we may have to schedule virtual meetings around home renovations!

The thing is, everything costs more than it used to. Many of my clients have saved up money to do those home renovations when they retire, only to find out the estimate is more than they expected—by a lot. This is why it's important to keep in touch about your plans with a financial professional such as myself. If you have your heart set on remodeling the kitchen, it may mean sacrifices in other areas—not taking the annual cruise you and your spouse had counted on that year, at least. During the pandemic, inflation in general and costs associated with home improvements rose significantly due to supply chain issues and the fact that so many people were engaging in home renovation projects. While the rate of inflation has receded since the pandemic, concerns around potential price increases from tariffs have led some of my clients—and me, I have to say—to accel-erate our home renovation projects before prices rise any further.

In retirement we all like to help out our families with our time and money, when we can. It's a natural impulse but also something to watch out for, because it can be taken to extremes. One example of this tendency, which I deal with in the practice, might go like this. There's a hypothetical example of Paul, who is currently living in Charlotte, North Carolina. He retired from his well-paying job after 30 years, and his life began to revolve around his daughter and grand-children. She had just gotten divorced from her husband and at the same time decided to change careers by going to nursing school. The divorce was financially devastating, as are many divorces in terms of having to form two households where one previously existed. Going back to school not only involved forgoing employment income, it also meant paying tuition, fees, books, etc.

My hypothetical client made the well-meaning decision to spend a lot of time with his family in retirement, but even more than time, what that meant was spending his retirement income on his daughter's rent, car lease, nursing school tuition, and more. When his grandkids called him and asked if he was hungry, that was a signal that he should take everyone out for an expensive dinner. He became responsible for taking his teenage granddaughter to school because his daughter had classes, but he wanted a day off now and then. Once she turned age 16, she started getting wild ideas of independence. Bam—now he's paying leases on three cars—his car, his daughter's car and his granddaughter's car. He was already paying for the whole family's cell phones—and everyone always wanted to upgrade to the latest and greatest iPhone.

Obviously, this client would have to adjust financially. I would tell him that if he kept spending at this rate, he would have to go back to work. He didn't want to do that, so instead he could sell his house and move in his with his daughter and her kids, which at least meant that he wouldn't be paying utilities, cable, taxes, etc. on two places. He sold one of his cars so he could get something more family-oriented. At that point, I might say, "What? You're in retirement! Your car isn't supposed to be family friendly!"

The problem with this type of client is that they don't have boundaries or set expectations regarding family support or generosity. Over-generosity in retirement isn't a problem in just this case. Too many newly retired grandparents in our society fear a loss of access to their grandchildren if they don't continue to be Daddy (or Mommy) Warbucks. With clients like these, I often find it necessary to script out with them conversations about how their children and grandchildren have financial responsibility to them, as well.

Sometimes it's not just your kids and grandkids calling on your resources. Many retirees might have a parent still living, or a sibling who's never been quite right financially. My own mother-in-law is still with us, fortunately, but she has a way of guilt-tripping my husband for money. "I took care of you, now it's your turn." I see this with some of my clients too. And I give them the same advice I give my husband: If you have the money and want to give it, then fine. It's a gift, not money you can expect to be paid back. If you don't have the money, then the answer is bleak, but obvious.

There are lots of potential problems for retirement finances here. What are the solutions?

The absolute first thing to resolve in retirement planning is how much money you have, or are going to have, and is it going to last 20 to 30 years? When I ask clients this at an initial meeting, most of them will raise their eyebrows and say something like, "Oh Lord, I don't know." That's why we do the meeting: to round up and build out the sources of retirement income.

You should look at it like this: Are you financially ready to be unemployed for the next several decades? Most people haven't thought of it this way, but that's the challenge—to replace the income they had from work with a "retirement paycheck" that comes from various sources like savings, a pension (if you're lucky enough to have one), Social Security, investments such as stocks, annuities, precious metals, etc.

This is where strategy comes in handy. We are all entitled to Social Security, but when is the best time to claim it? As we know, the earlier you claim, the less money you receive. If you have your health at age 65, it might be better to continue working for that part of your retirement paycheck and then have access to the greater benefit once you fully retire, say at age 70. You can of course keep working after claiming Social Security, but there are strict earnings limits if you claim Social Security before your full retirement age, which will temporarily reduce your Social Security benefit.[5] If you turned age 62 in 2025—or are younger than age 62 in 2025—your full retirement age is 67.[6]

Your retirement age, and when to claim Social Security, are highly dependent upon your financial situation and also your health. If

---

5. "What happens if I work and get Social Security Retirement Benefits?" U.S. Social Security Administration, Jan. 2, 2025, https://www.ssa.gov/faqs/en/questions/KA-01921.html

6. "What is full retirement age?" U.S. Social Security Administration, Jan. 2, 2025, https://www.ssa.gov/faqs/en/questions/KA-01885.html

you have physically labored your entire life at a job in a factory, for example, your body may not be capable of working beyond your early 60s. Others who have a desk job may need to and be able to work longer. Social Security claiming, which we will discuss in more detail in Chapter 6, isn't the only aspect of your retirement that benefits from strategic thinking with a financial planner. Healthcare is a big one—if you're enrolled in Medicare, well, surcharges might kick in if you're earning above a certain amount.

Most people have some sort of retirement savings account, often through their current or former employer. That's what replaced pensions in the U.S. I'm a strong advocate for all of my clients getting control over the money they have saved through working. You want to have that money accessible to you. In uncertain—to say the least—economic times, you don't want, for example, to be over-invested in your company's stock. You likely remember what happened to the employees of Enron who were heavily invested in their company's stock—they lost their jobs at the same time that the company went belly up and their shares became worthless.[7]

So, let's say you do have a relatively well-stocked IRA or 401(k). Most retirement accounts require you to start taking minimum distributions (RMDs) once you hit age 73, whether you need the income or not.[8] And, unless you've already converted some or all of your traditional IRA or 401(k) into a Roth, your RMDs will be taxed at the same rate as regular income.[9] Receiving RMDs could even put you in a higher tax bracket.

---

7. "When ESOPs Go Wrong: The Enron Scandal," VestedFinance.com, Jan. 31, 2025, https://vestedfinance.com/blog/us-stocks/when-esops-go-wrong-the-enron-scandal/"Retirement plan and IRA required minimum distributions FAQs," U.S. Internal Revenue Service, March 13, 2025, https://www.irs.gov/retirement-plans/retirement-plan-and-ira-required-minimum-distributions-faqs#

8. "Retirement plan and IRA required minimum distributions FAQs," U.S. Internal Revenue Service, March 13, 2025, https://www.irs.gov/retirement-plans/retirement-plan-and-ira-required-minimum-distributions-faqs#

9. "Retirement plan and IRA required minimum distributions FAQs," U.S. Internal Revenue Service, March 13, 2025, https://www.irs.gov/retirement-plans/retirement-plan-and-ira-required-minimum-distributions-faqs#

A strategy for mitigating retirement taxes is therefore one of the tools that any competent retirement financial planner will have access to, joined with a strategy for when to claim Social Security (if you're married, it can be advantageous to claim at different times), and a strategy for when to start taking distributions from your retirement savings account(s). Together, this is what I referred to earlier as your "retirement paycheck" and represents your various income streams in retirement.

Establishing these income sources first helps you to create a spending plan when there ideally is extra money available for bigger expenses—the kitchen remodel you had your heart set on and the new car you're likely to need at some point. An important aspect of your retirement income is a strategy that helps mitigate taxes throughout retirement. This typically involves tax diversification—a strategy that accounts for the various tax treatments of the different accounts you'll be withdrawing from, as well as their RMD rules. This works in three stages:

1. During your *working years*, you are likely making tax-deferred contributions to a qualified retirement plan. If your employer matches, you want to contribute enough to get the full amount. Consider an HSA to invest for retirement healthcare expenses. Leverage Roth accounts if they're available—that money will be taxed now, not in retirement when you can probably afford it less.
2. In the *immediate pre-retirement years*, you can look into converting your retirement assets into a Roth 401(k) or Roth IRA when the market is down and your income is lower to help reduce the amount of taxable income in retirement, and potentially forego RMD obligations. If you have highly appreciated employer securities in your account, you might look into converting them to be taxed as long-term capital gains. Keep in mind, Roth conversions mean paying taxes on these funds now, ideally from sources outside of your qualified retirement plan. A conversion will affect your

income tax rate in the year of the conversion, and may affect other areas of your financial plan, such as increased Medicare premiums, so be sure to work with your financial and tax advisors on this.

3. *During retirement*, you should think strategically about distributions. It might be advantageous for you to take distributions from a tax-deferred account before you are required to, if delaying will put you in a higher tax bracket. Once you're age 70 ½ you can, if you are able, also give money to qualified charities for tax advantages, and these will count toward your RMD.[10]

Finally, plan proactively for the retirement risks that I discussed in earlier chapters: interest rate risk, investment risk, and loss of a spouse risk. This last one is important, especially for women, who tend to live longer than men in the U.S., by more than five years on average.[11]

HEALTHCARE READINESS

When you're in pre-retirement, you might be as healthy as you're going to get. It's time therefore to assess the current state of your health as a way to project how much care you're likely to need in retirement.

As planners, especially when talking about healthcare needs, we talk about three stages in retirement. The Go-Go Years are your most active. You have the time and money to take frequent vacations and be active to a great extent with your hobbies or continued work. As your health starts to decline, you enter the Slow-Go Years. You're less active. If you worked part-time up till now, it's probably advisable to stop, and the trips you take aren't cruises around the world but shorter trips to

10. "Tax Diversification: A Strategy to Help Your Retirement Assets Last," Ameriprise, https://www.ameriprise.com/financial-goals-priorities/taxes/tax-diversification-retire ment

11. "Do Women Live Longer than Men in the U.S.?" USA Facts, Mar. 21, 2025: https:// usafacts.org/articles/do-women-live-longer-than-men-in-the-us.

see your kids and grandkids. Finally, the No-Go Years are the last phase of retirement, where your (lack of) health may keep you confined to home most of the time and you start to require things like long-term care, a home health aide, and support from your family.

Your health insurance coverage needs to be enough to meet your healthcare needs at every stage of your retirement journey. You need to start considering more the potential cost of healthcare, especially ongoing costs like deductibles, co-pays, co-insurance, and out-of-pocket costs. Healthcare costs have consistently run ahead of inflation since the new millennium.[12]

Good thing you'll have Medicare, right? Well, yes, but that requires some planning too. Original Medicare is run by the government and covers hospital stays (Part A) and everything else (Part B) except for medications (Part D), for which you need a separate plan. Many people who go this route end up combining Original Medicare with a Medicare Supplement insurance policy, also referred to as Medigap—which is insurance that covers the shortfall. Or you can opt for Medicare Advantage (Part C) which are private plans that bundle the services of Parts A, B and D with extra benefits and coverage for dental, hearing and vision, and often prescription drugs as well.

With Medicare, you can only enroll at certain times of the year, unless you have a qualifying life event.[13] Also, the various Medicare Advantage plans have different deductibles, premiums, co-pays ranging from very low coverage with very low premiums and higher coverage with higher premiums, all of which needs to be taken into account along with your financial situation and health readiness to retire.

---

12. "How Does Medical Inflation Compare to Inflation in the Rest of the Economy?" Peterson-KFF Health System Tracker, Aug. 2, 2024: https://www.healthsystemtracker. org/brief/how-does-medical-inflation-compare-to-inflation-in-the-rest-of-the-econ omy/#

13. "Medicare Advantage vs. Medigap with Original Medicare: What Are the Differences and How to Choose," GoodRx, Apr. 5, 2024, https://www.goodrx.com/insurance/ medicare/medicare-advantage-vs-medigap

What if you retire before you become eligible for Medicare at age 65? Some of my clients do face the "healthcare gap" between when they retire and age 65 and need to get insurance to bridge the gap, unless you're among the lucky few whose former employers will carry their coverage. Most of us must go to the ACA marketplace and find a plan, which has plenty of challenges. While working, you're used to just having a couple health insurance options, but now you have to figure out comparing deductibles and co-pays on the Exchange, with its Platinum, Gold, Silver and Bronze-level plans and measure them against what you're likely to need in early retirement. Whatever you choose, you'll have to factor in around $800-$1200 a month, if you don't have any subsidies per month to bridge the gap.[14]

Then there is long-term care. Again, no one wants to think about the No-Go Years because in terms of health this involves losing independence, needing bouts of long-term care, and eventual end-of-life care. It seems crass to put price tags on these things, but it must be done.

Long-term care insurance can be expensive, especially as you get older, and premiums increase. Since Medicare doesn't cover it, those who can afford it are forced to look at traditional insurance, combination LTC/insurance policies or annuities. Standalone long-term care insurance can be challenging to find.[15] To get a reasonable rate you need to purchase the policy when you're younger, and it helps to apply as a couple, but most of my clients probably didn't think that far ahead. Then there are insurance and annuity policies with a long-term care component (which offers just limited coverage), Health Savings Accounts that you can use for long-term care and other options.[16]

---

14. "Retiring at 62 or Before? Average Early Retirement Health Costs + 9 Ways to Afford Insurance," March 26, 2025, https://www.boldin.com/retirement/retiring-at-62-early-retirement-health-costs.

15. "Retiring at 62 or Before? Average Early Retirement Health Costs + 9 Ways to Afford Insurance," March 26, 2025, https://www.boldin.com/retirement/retiring-at-62-early-retirement-health-costs

16. "How to Pay for Long-Term Care," Kiplinger, Apr. 10, 2025, https://www.kiplinger. com/retirement/long-term-care/how-to-pay-for-long-term-care

What I'm describing is some of the results of long, hard conversations I had with my clients. Many people don't know these things, and to the extent they do, they try to avoid thinking about them. But you have to have the hard conversations: What happens if I live into my 90s? What if this happens and my mind is gone? By this point, you won't be able to make decisions for yourself, which leaves others to make the best decisions for you amongst a potentially limited set of options. It's always better to have the hard conversation with your family, your financial advisor and legal counsel, than to have left things unclear which could lead to everyone suffering.

READINESS STRATEGIES FOR SMALL BUSINESS OWNERS

Within the universe of aligning your retirement journey with your retirement readiness, there are some special considerations for small business owners. For many of my small business owner clients, their business represents their biggest retirement savings asset. In other words, the value of their business is a significant part of their retirement plan. That means it's critical to plan for a business transition well before the date you, the small business owner, want to retire. To gain the liquid assets you need to retire well, you need to somehow realize at least part of the value of your business in cash.

Proactively considering how you plan to monetize your business interests can bring clarity to retirement planning. Are your children interested in taking the business over? Do you have internal senior staff who may be interested in buying out your business from you over time? Or do you plan to sell to an external party, such as a venture capitalist, private equity firm or larger player in your industry?

You also need to think about what your role will be during and after this transition. Do you want to continue to work for the business either as an employee or a consultant? Let's look at this example. Consider a situation where a dentist with a practice that has 25 employees is considering either an internal buy-out from her two associate dentists or an external buyout. After the sale, she would like to work solely as a dentist for the practice, eventually exiting and fully retiring after 18 months.

Deciding how you are going to access the retirement assets tied up in your business and what role—if any—you will play in the business after the sale are the kinds of decisions you need to make—with the help of an experienced financial advisor such as myself.

READINESS STRATEGIES FOR SINGLE WOMEN

Single women are another group that faces a different situation from the typical retiree, who is usually part of a couple. Whether you have always been single–or are single because of a divorce or the death of a spouse–there are issues that require special consideration to retire well.

Among these issues are the fact that you will be funding your retirement solely from your own assets and income. With that comes the freedom to make all the decisions yourself, in your own best interest. You don't have to consider what is best for a spouse, you only have to decide what is best for you. You also have to consider issues around long-term care, since you won't necessarily have a spouse who can take care of you.

Many single women are in an enviable position in that they have diligently saved and are in the position to have a work-optional lifestyle if they so desire. That means you won't have to work because you need the money now or in retirement, but instead you can enjoy work for the other benefits it provides such as mental stimulation and challenges, friendships and more—or not.

Having these more nuanced conversations with someone who understands your financial situation and your goals and supports your desire for a sustainable retirement is important.

UP NEXT

Now that you've gained some understanding of your ideal retirement journey, have evaluated your retirement readiness and have aligned your journey with your readiness, it's time to learn about the steps involved in creating a retirement plan. This is where you will learn about the nuts and bolts of implementing an investment strategy, crafting a Social Security Strategy, building a tax strategy, and creating a retirement income stream.

4

RETIRING YOUR WAY

The process of crafting and implementing a retirement income plan is crucial in building a sustainable retirement so you and your spouse—if you have one—can embark on your unique retirement journey. As we've discussed in earlier chapters, your retirement income plan is based upon how you want that journey to look and the resources you bring to support that journey.

In this chapter, you'll learn about the different components of a retirement income plan. To carry out your plan, we need to implement an investment strategy, build a tax strategy, help reduce risk and create a retirement income stream. Obviously, the details for each couple's retirement income plan are different, but the overall strategy is generally the same. I'll walk you through how I strategically analyze and plan each part of the retirement journey, so you can understand how it works and why it is important.

IMPLEMENTING AN INVESTMENT STRATEGY

The retirement planning process is always individualized, not only because it feels better that way but because different people have different goals for retirement, and the job of that trusted advisor is to figure out how to make that happen with the resources available. While the goals are interrelated, one primary driver of the entire strategy is risk tolerance.

To help simplify the process of determining risk tolerance, I use what is known as the Rule of 100.[1] The Rule of 100 subtracts your age from 100 to set the allocation of risky assets such as stocks in your retirement income portfolio. That means if you are age 62, you subtract 62 from 100 and get 38. Then, roughly 38% of your portfolio would be invested in the stock market. As you get older, the percentage of assets allocated to the stock market gradually declines. Keep in mind, this is a rule of thumb only and needs to be customized to every individual based on their specific goals, assets, and risk tolerance.

Over time, that means your exposure to the stock market goes down. That decline coincides with you entering an era in your life where you generally want less exposure to risk and more certainty around income. With the Rule of 100 in place, your retirement is positioned to decrease your risk as you get older.

With a set part of your assets invested in risky assets in the stock market, the rest of your assets will be invested in assets designed to produce lifetime income or play another role, such as hedge against inflation. These more risk-oriented assets, which will be explored in more depth in Chapter 5, may include things like stocks, precious metals such as gold, and bonds and bond funds. Of key importance is creating a source of guaranteed income from your existing resources—your nest egg, so to speak. And alongside that guaranteed income, the other priority is to plot a path towards accomplishing the longer-term retirement goals, including mitigating risks such as inflation, long-term care, death of a spouse risk, and more.

---

1. "Should Retirees Follow the '100 Minus Your Age' Rule?" SmartAsset, Dec. 10, 2024, https://smartasset.com/retirement/rule-of-100-investing

BUILDING A TAX STRATEGY

When retirees are planning their retirement, there is often a bias towards the eye-popping sums of income certain strategies can theoretically produce. Far more important, however, is the balance between the income a strategy produces versus how much of that income the retiree will get to hold onto. As I always say, "It's not what you have—it's what you keep."

Many people expect that their taxes will be lower in retirement, which is not necessarily the case. That's one reason why people who are farther away from retirement may have a better chance for tax diversification than those who are just about to retire. It's not that you can't diversify for taxation right before retirement—it's that there are more options if you are farther away from retirement, as you will learn later.

Different types of investments, and different types of investment accounts, have different amounts of exposure to taxation, and within that dynamic these differential exposures will vary depending on your specific situation. How much you take home from the investment products you buy varies based on how tax efficient they are, where you live, your age, and so on.

A key aspect involved in reducing the tax burden on your income when you retire is the process of diversification through taxability. As you'll learn in this chapter and in Chapter 5, whether you pay taxes and how much you pay in taxes is largely dependent upon the type of retirement accounts you have. Tax diversification is the process of spreading your retirement assets across accounts that have different taxation.

Here's an overview of the most common types of retirement accounts and how they are taxed:[2]

- **Traditional IRA and 401(k):** You receive a tax deduction when you contribute to a traditional IRA or 401(k). You pay

2. "Tax-efficient investing: A beginner's guide," Investopedia.com, March 31, 2025, https://www.investopedia.com/articles/stocks/11/intro-tax-efficient-investing.asp

taxes at ordinary income rates when you withdraw funds in retirement, and a 10% IRS penalty for withdrawals before age 59-1/2.

- **Brokerage account:** You pay taxes when you sell securities such as stocks, bonds, mutual funds or ETFs at a gain, as well as when you receive interest, dividends and other types of income each year.
- **Bank or credit union account:** You pay taxes on any interest you receive on your savings or money market savings accounts each year.
- **Roth IRA:** You contribute to a Roth with after-tax income. Since you have already paid taxes, there are no taxes due upon withdrawal once you reach age 59-1/2 and the account has been open for at least five years.
- **Health Savings Account (HSA):** HSAs are the only triple-tax free account. You receive a tax deduction when you contribute, can withdraw the funds tax free when used for qualified medical expenses and any interest or dividend income or profit from securities sales are tax free within the account. Withdrawals for non-qualified expenses will be taxed as ordinary income and may also incur a 10% IRS penalty.

If you're like many of my pre-retiree clients, you probably have most of your retirement assets in tax-deferred accounts such as traditional IRAs or 401(k)s. You likely have enjoyed the opportunity to reduce your current taxable income with your retirement plan contributions. But when you withdraw those funds in retirement, you will have to pay taxes at ordinary income rates, which may increase at some point in retirement.

With these types of tax-deferred accounts, you also must begin taking required minimum distributions (RMDs) at either age 73, if you turn age 73 before Jan. 1, 2033, or at age 75, if you turn age 75 on or after Jan. 1, 2033.[3]

To help increase tax diversification in retirement, you may want to convert some of your traditional IRA savings into a Roth IRA. To make a Roth conversion, as they are known, will mean that you will need to pay the taxes due on the amount you convert at the time you convert.[4] We'll discuss the specifics of this strategy more in Chapter 5. Roth IRAs can be a good tool for tax diversification because qualified withdrawals aren't taxable.

Saving money in a brokerage account is an attractive option for many as taxes are only due when you receive interest, dividends or other payouts or sell securities at a profit. There are no limits on contributions, no distribution requirements and no penalties for withdrawing early.

When used for medical expenses, qualified withdrawals from Health Savings Accounts are tax-free, which can be very useful in retirement. That's because retirement can carry many health care expenses, from Medicare premiums, co-pays and deductibles to long-term care costs. You can also invest the savings in your HSA so that it can grow in retirement. That way you could use it for healthcare expenses in late retirement, when they are likely to be higher.

The ultimate goal is not to focus on one type of account at the expense of others, but to identify the right mix of accounts for each client and family. Taxation will play a significant role in this determination process. The point is to create flexibility through taxation, so there is more ability to be dynamic and respond to material and market circumstances. You want to be able to adapt no matter what

---

3. "SECURE 2.0 Act Summary: New Retirement Savings Changes to Know," March 21, 2025, https://www.kiplinger.com/retirement/bipartisan-retirement-savings-package-in-massive-budget-bill

4. "Retirement plans FAQs regarding IRAs," U.S. Internal Revenue Service, Nov. 15, 2024, https://www.irs.gov/retirement-plans/retirement-plans-faqs-regarding-iras

situation arises in your home or the economy of the country and the world.

One way that I like to look at tax diversification is through the lens of green, red and yellow money.

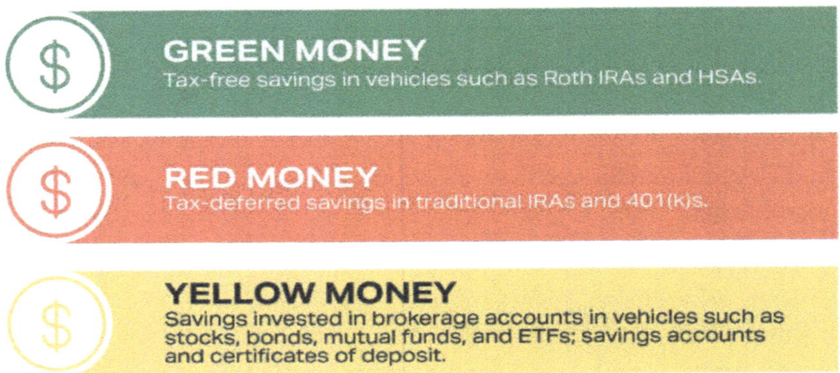

Bank products are FDIC-insured up to applicable limits, whereas investments are subject to risk, including possible loss of principal. Insurance guarantees are backed by the financial strength and claims-paying ability of the issuing company. Roth distributions are tax free after age 59-1/2 and the account has been open for at least five years. HSA funds are tax-free for qualified medical expenses. Distributions from tax-deferred vehicles are subject to ordinary income taxes and may incur an additional 10% IRS penalty before age 59-1/2.

Along with tax diversification, you can also consider diversifying your assets in various ways as the following example shows.

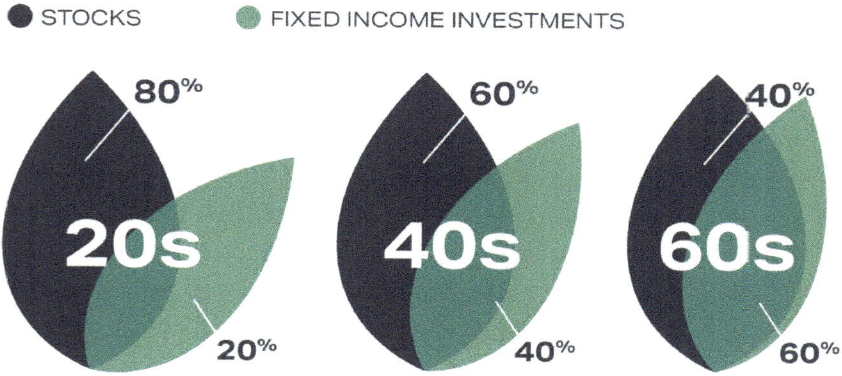

This information is for illustrative purposes only and does not constitute a recommendation or advice for your particular circumstances. Your portfolio allocation will vary, perhaps significantly based on your unique financial situation and needs.

In our analysis, we collate a statement to demonstrate the different streams of retirement income, dividing them into green money, yellow money, and red money. You may find that, like many other pre-retirees, you have a high percentage of your savings in red money. Many of the clients I work with are hard workers who have saved diligently but now are in a position where they might have to pay more taxes than is optimal if they don't take steps to diversify by taxability.

Diversification by taxability can sound like an easy proposition, until you examine all of the factors, many of which are not necessarily well understood. This is why we opt for a process-driven approach to taxation, because using a tool for comprehensive analysis helps us optimize the entire process. Otherwise, retirement can quickly become like gambling—a game of luck rather than skill.

REDUCING RISK

Retiring without a comprehensive approach to tax liability is not the only type of risk, however. Insurance products are available to help protect against some of the big issues a retiree or couple can run into throughout the process of retiring and spending the rest of their lives in that retirement.

There are insurance (leverage) policies that can not only provide potential retirement income, but that can also help you achieve other retirement goals such as your legacy goals and that may also serve to help mitigate your taxes. These kinds of insurance policies allow you to leverage your resources to achieve a variety of retirement-related goals. Withdrawals from whole life/universal life insurance policies, for example, are considered loans and are therefore free from income taxes[5,6].

In addition, with these types of policies, the amount of premium you can pay into them isn't subject to limits that IRAs and Roth IRAs are subject to, which is an example of leverage. These policies may help you to accumulate cash value that can help protect you from volatility.[7]

CREATING A RETIREMENT INCOME STREAM

The key to creating a retirement income stream is to replace your paycheck through Social Security and through income from other financial and investment products. While Social Security can seem simple in that you and your employer contribute money through your paycheck and then you receive a stream of income in retirement, there are a dizzying array of strategies that you can use to claim Social Security.

---

5. Policy loans and withdrawals will reduce available cash values and death benefits and may cause the policy to lapse or affect any guarantees against lapse. Additional premium payments may be required to keep the policy in force. In the event of a lapse, outstanding policy loans in excess of unrecovered cost basis will be subject to ordinary income tax. Tax laws are subject to change. You should consult a tax professional.

6. "Whole Life Insurance: A Multipurpose Financial Planning Tool," Kiplinger.com, April 24, 2024, https://www.kiplinger.com/article/retirement/t034-c032-s014-using-whole-life-insurance-for-your-financial-plan.html

7. "Whole Life Insurance: A Multipurpose Financial Planning Tool," Kiplinger.com, April 24, 2024, https://www.kiplinger.com/article/retirement/t034-c032-s014-using-whole-life-insurance-for-your-financial-plan.html

Obviously for couples the considerations are more complex. Many of the clients I work with are couples where the man is older and has been the primary breadwinner during working years. This situation commonly has a few key considerations. The man being the primary breadwinner means that the woman likely had less income in comparison, and thus her Social Security payments will be much smaller over the entire length of retirement. Additionally, for a variety of reasons including life expectancy and a relative age difference to begin with, often the man will be the one in the couple to pass away first. It also becomes complicated by how much spousal benefits could benefit the spouse of the breadwinner.

We use these factors, among others, to give you the options so that you can make the optimal decision for the retirement that you and your spouse have been dreaming of. Besides spousal benefits, there are also survivor benefits for spouses of individuals who passed away before claiming Social Security and divorced spouse benefits. If your spouse passes away during retirement, you as the surviving spouse will receive the higher Social Security benefit automatically.[8] If, for example, the higher earning husband had a monthly Social Security benefit of $3,000 while you had a benefit of $1,000 a month, you will receive the higher benefit, and your benefit will be discontinued. I'll provide more specific information on Social Security in coming chapters.

This is why I will be sure to make a provision in your retirement income plan to address this potential drop in income. You don't want your spouse to suffer a decline in their standard of living when you pass, a point that most of my clients are adamant about.

Besides Social Security, you can create streams of income through other financial products such as annuities, including fixed-indexed annuities, which we will discuss more in Chapter 5. You may have other sources of income that include a side business, part-time work, rental properties or more.

---

8. "How does Social Security work when a spouse dies?" AARP.org, March 31, 2025, https://www.aarp.org/social-security/faq/when-spouse-dies/

Maybe you've always dreamed of starting a business when you were laboring away at your 9-5 job and you do so in retirement, generating income—that's an income stream. Perhaps you bought a condo for your child when they were attending college and now you can rent that out for income. Or maybe, like some of my clients, you have several rental properties, and you plan on building up that business in retirement. Maybe you do some consulting with your former employer, or you restore antique cars and sell them once the restoration is done—that's more incoming money that you can add to your income stream. You may have a pension that you can draw on when you retire, which is a kind of red money, because pensions are taxable.

The whole point of this aspect of retirement income planning is to combine many different sources of income to replace the dollars and cents that showed up on your paycheck. This is not going to represent the exact amount on a stable 40-hour a week job because in retirement you will have a different set of expenses that you need to cover. The point is to have guaranteed income that covers your expenses and the various contingencies that can arise in retirement such as health issues, home repairs and helping your family.

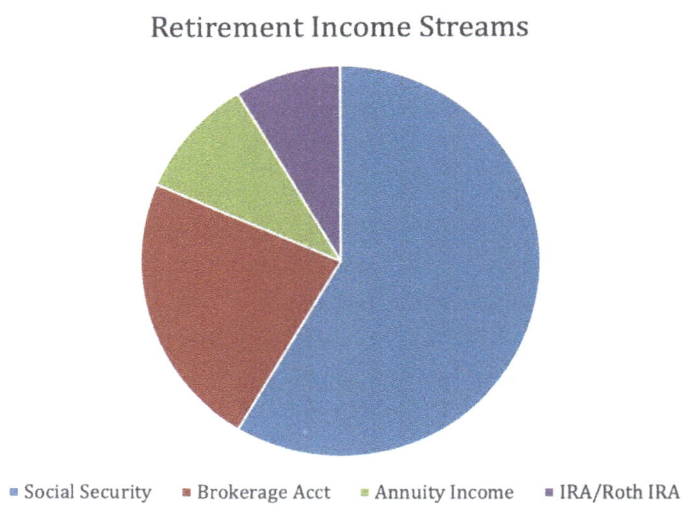

Hypothetical example shown for illustrative purposes only. It is not a recommendation or advice for your specific situation; your portfolio allocation and income sources will vary by your unique needs and objectives.

OTHER CONSIDERATIONS

Some retirees have highly specialized situations that can significantly alter the analysis and its results. This group includes independent women, people who did not have access to workplace retirement plans and business owners.

Individuals, and especially women who do not have a partner they plan to retire with, tend to have less income and savings but a similar amount of expenses in retirement to a couple who retires together and can have fewer tax advantages. Without multiple forms of income due to being in a couple, a single person should plan more carefully regarding contingencies and long-term care solutions. Again, the priority is not to find a silver bullet; it is to envision the retirement you want and figure out how to do that by replacing that paycheck with other forms of income. Independent women may have to look closely at other alternative investment opportunities for income, save more or work longer to have the type of lifestyle they want in retirement.

If you worked for a small company or are an independent contractor, you have challenges in saving for retirement that your peers who are employed by larger companies with 401(k) plans and 401(k) matches may not have to face. Many small companies don't offer company-sponsored retirement plans.

If you are a self-employed independent contractor, you need to find ways to save even while you are paying both sides of your Social Security and Medicare taxes.[9] Fortunately, there are a number

---

9. "Self-employment tax (Social Security and Medicare taxes)," U.S. Internal Revenue Service, Nov. 25, 2024, https://www.irs.gov/businesses/small-businesses-self-employed/ self-employment-tax-social-security-and-medicare-taxes

of accounts that you can set up through brokerages to save for retirement, including SEP-IRAs and a Solo 401(k). You can also open your own bank accounts and other assets to help create tax-efficient retirement income.

Business owners, single or married, have a unique set of circumstances that require their own set of calculations to make the best decisions about succession planning versus selling the business. A lot of this depends on market and industry factors, but the necessity here is to figure out how these pieces fit together. How does the income from the sale of the business or the succession plan affect the distribution of assets?

If the business is to be sold, in some industries it is common for the owner to stay on as an employee and gradually transfer their equity over time. The paycheck is income; the equity transfers are income. For succession planning, I may suggest that your beneficia-ries rely upon the proceeds of a life insurance policy as appropriate, and that we can use other assets to create a retirement income plan to help you live your ideal retirement.

UP NEXT

Now that you understand how the pieces of the retirement income plan fit together, we will take a deeper dive into how you might set up your investments in Chapter 5.

5

EXECUTING YOUR INVESTMENT STRATEGY

Now that we've gone through the steps to develop a retirement income plan based on your retirement journey goals, it's time to create an investment strategy based on that plan. While your retirement income plan is the foundation of your retirement journey, the investment strategy is the nuts and bolts of how you invest your money to bring that plan to fruition. Whatever the source of your retirement income is—retirement accounts such as IRAs, Social Security, rental property income, consulting work—my job is to help you turn those sources of funds into a cohesive and coherent investment strategy that carries out the objectives of your plan.

Most of my clients leave our planning meetings encouraged, because I'm upfront with them about how we plan for retirement income. I don't tell my clients that they can live in the style of King Charles, but I also don't tell them that they must save some unreasonable amount in the millions to be able to retire at all. Because most people are not King Charles, but conversely, most people have some resources that enable us first to plan your retirement journey, and then to create an investment strategy to help carry out that plan. My job is to make sure you understand that plan and the subsequent strategy, are involved in it, and are invested in it

This chapter will examine the essential defining features of an investment strategy, how to determine your tolerance for risk and asset allocation, how fixed-income strategies such as annuities can create guaranteed income from your retirement nest egg that helps to fulfill your plan, and investing for the achievement of long-term goals in retirement.

WHAT IS AN INVESTMENT STRATEGY?

An investment strategy defines how your money will be invested based on your goals. In retirement, your goal is to replace your work paycheck with the lowest amount of risk possible to your assets. An investment strategy is not set in stone—instead, it is a document that can be refined over time as external or internal circumstances change.[1]

An investment strategy guides your decision-making around investing throughout your retirement. The objective is to never have questions about how you will achieve your retirement financial goals, because with me, you'll have an investment strategy that you are comfortable with, because you not only fully understand it, but you also believe in it. We do this, first, to help create consistency so that you aren't chasing big returns or investing in other ways that are contrary to your goals, and second, to help protect you financially from external events and life changes.

Over the long term (which retirement is), holding a diversified[2] portfolio is intended to help reduce risk (which is the name of the game).[3] That means putting together the different diversified building blocks of a portfolio, which might include stocks, annuities, precious

---

1. "How to Define an Investment Strategy," Morningstar, May 5, 2024: https://www. morningstar.com.au/personal-finance/how-to-define-an-investment-strategy.

2. Neither diversification nor asset allocation not ensure a profit or guarantee against losses.

3. "6 Steps to Building a Long-Term Investment Strategy," Fidelity Wealth Manage-ment, March 7, 2025, https://www.fidelity.com/learning-center/wealth-management-insights/6-steps-to-building-an-investment-strategy

metals, bonds and insurance, to create a strategy to help carry out a retirement income plan. Different asset classes can perform differently under various economic conditions, and a diversified portfolio helps mitigate risk, which I help enforce through rebalancing. This helps ensure that your asset allocation stays on track.[4] Asset allocation is the practice of dividing your assets among different investments and products to help reduce risk. Sure, if you want a small amount of money to play around and invest on your own, that's not a problem, but those funds won't be counted on to fund your everyday retirement needs. Below are historical average annual returns by investment class:

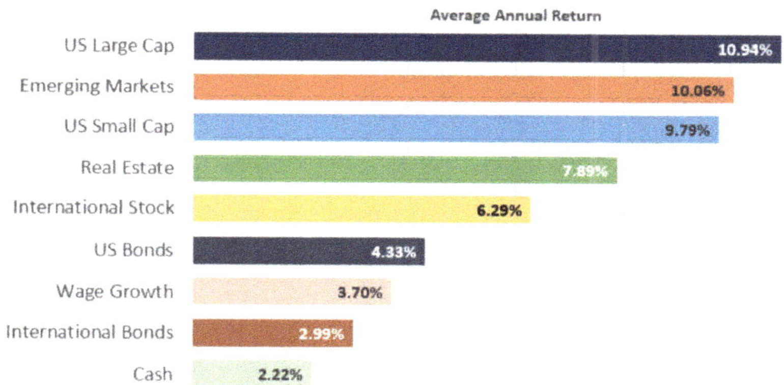

Source: Bloomberg

For illustrative and educational purposes only. Not investment advice or a solicitation to buy or sell any security. Past performance is not indicative of future results.

Index returns reflect average annual total returns from each index's respective inception date through 12/31/2025. Returns are gross of fees and do not reflect the deduction of advisory fees, transaction costs, or other

---

4. "6 Steps to Building a Long-Term Investment Strategy," Fidelity Wealth Management, March 7, 2025, https://www.fidelity.com/learning-center/wealth-management-insights/6-steps-to-building-an-investment-strategy

expenses, which would reduce returns shown. Indices are unmanaged and not available for direct investment.

The indices represented include:

- *MSCI USA Large Cap (inception date 6/1/1994)*
- *MSCI Emerging Markets (inception date 12/31/1987)*
- *MSCI USA Small Cap (inception date 6/1/1994)*
- *S&P 1500 Real Estate (Sector) Total Return (inception date 10/9/2001)*
- *MSCI ACWI ex USA Total Return (inception date 9/30/1994)*
- *Bloomberg US Aggregate (inception date 3/31/1997)*
- *Bloomberg Global Aggregate (inception date 8/20/2001)*
- *Bloomberg US Treasury Bills 1–3 Month (inception date 1/4/1999)*
- *Bloomberg Commodity Index Total Return (inception date 5/19/1997)*

Each index has a different inception date. Returns are not measured over a common time period and are therefore not directly comparable to one another. The Wage Growth Tracker is included as a proxy for wage growth and is not an investable index.

Investing involves risk, including the possible loss of principal. Equity investments are subject to market volatility. International and emerging market investments carry additional risks including currency fluctuation, geopolitical risk, and differing regulatory environments. Fixed income investments are subject to interest rate and credit risk. Real estate investments are subject to liquidity and economic risks. Commodity investments may experience greater volatility than traditional asset classes.

WHY AN INVESTMENT STRATEGY IS IMPORTANT

An investment strategy sets the parameters around how you will execute your retirement income plan from an investment point of view. The reason why an investment strategy is important is because it creates a framework for how you will invest. If in the future you wonder why you have the specific investment and product portfolio that you have, you can refer to that investment strategy within your plan for a rationale. You can use that information to explain your strategy to your children, grandchildren, friends, coworkers or anyone else who is interested in the reasons behind your plan and strategy. From a coherent and consistent investment strategy, investment returns are designed to support your retirement plan through total return, interest, dividends and income from other sources.

Having a retirement income plan and investment strategy helps keep you aligned with the purpose of your retirement journey. When you buy into this holistic process, you're able to let go of potentially harmful behaviors that could sabotage your success. There are several "investor biases" that result in behavior that can undermine the objectives you have for your retirement journey.

For example, you might fall prey to recency bias, in which you believe that because the market has performed well recently, it will continue to do so in the future, leading you to be overly optimistic about the performance of your investments.[5] Or, you might suffer from first impression bias, in which your early experiences as an investor color your investing behavior going forward. If, for example, you began investing during the Great Recession when markets were severely battered, you might act as if the market is going to tank at any moment, leading you to invest more conservatively than you need to.[6]

One of the most common investor biases is loss aversion, which means that losses are more painful and memorable than gains are pleasurable and memorable. That leads to the tendency to hold on to

---

5. "Improving investor outcomes by minimizing investor bias," Vanguard.com, May 14, 2024, https://corporate.vanguard.com/content/corporatesite/us/en/corp/articles/improving-investing-outcomes-minimizing-investor-bias.html

6. "Improving investor outcomes by minimizing investor bias," Vanguard.com, May 14, 2024, https://corporate.vanguard.com/content/corporatesite/us/en/corp/articles/improving-investing-outcomes-minimizing-investor-bias.html

securities that have lost value in the hope that they will regain what they have lost.[7] These biases can lead to emotional investing, which can be harmful to your investment strategy, your investment portfolio and your goals.

A recent report by Virtus Investment Partners has shown the impact of emotional decisions on investing. According to this report, during the 20-year period ending Dec. 31, 2024, the average stock fund investor under-performed the S&P 500 by 1.2 percentage points a year. For bond fund investors, the gap was even more, as they under-performed the Bloomberg Aggregate Bond Index by 3.3 percentage points over 20 years.[8]

When there is economic turmoil, especially during a recession when it seems like things won't get better, it can be tempting to change your investments and question your investment strategy and retirement income plan. Often, worry and fear drive those doubts. I always encourage my clients to call me or to come into the office so we can talk through their fears, and I can educate them on the potential value of sticking to the plan and strategy that we've established.

In 2025, when I was writing this book, President Trump's tariff announcements caused a significant amount of market volatility. In early April 2025, for example, the S&P 500 fell below 5,000 for the first time in nearly a year, wiping out trillions of dollars in investor's portfolios.[9] In 2020, early in the COVID-19 pandemic, stock markets experienced their three worst days since 1897 in the fastest bear market in nearly 100 years.[10]

---

7. "Improving investor outcomes by minimizing investor bias," Vanguard.com, May 14, 2024, https://corporate.vanguard.com/content/corporatesite/us/en/corp/articles/improving-investing-outcomes-minimizing-investor-bias.html

8. "Minds over Markets: A Behavioral Guide to Investing," Virtus Investment Partners, April 16, 2025, https://www.virtus.com/assets/files/35y/minds-over-market s_5500.pdf

9. "Why trade tensions are a 'storm cloud' over financial markets," World Economic Forum, April 17, 2025, https://www.weforum.org/stories/2025/04/tariffs-trade-tensions-storm-cloud-stocks-financial-markets/

10. "In the Markets Now: Investing Lessons from COVID," Baird Private Wealth Management, March 17, 2025, https://www.bairdwealth.com/insights/market-insights/baird-market-strategy/2025/03/in-the-markets-now-investing-lessons-from-covid/

In situations like these, it is easy for investors, especially those near retirement, to panic as they see their hard-earned savings evaporating. Those fears can lead to panic-related selling. Unfortunately, because the market moves so quickly these days due to algorithmic trading, by the time you pull the trigger on selling, the market may have already fallen.[11] Algorithmic trading uses programmed algorithms to execute stock market trades rapidly, much faster than human trading.[12]

Often, when investors sell in a panic, they miss out on subsequent rallies when the markets—and the economy—eventually recover. Like in 2020 and 2008, many of those who held on to their investments during the downturn eventually saw their investments recover, versus those who sold and stayed out of the market.[13] This goes double for retirement investing, which is by definition defensive and risk averse.[14]

Think of the people who sold their assets at the height of the crash in 2008, when the S&P 500 lost 57% of its value from previous heights, who missed out on the subsequent recovery.[15] Short-term price movements in one investment, sector, or the market generally, should never be confused with long-term value. You'll understand in becoming financially educated that all those negative numbers in the report are losses on paper. They aren't made real until you decide to

---

11. "Algorithmic Trading and Market Volatility: Impact of High-Frequency Trading," Michigan Journal of Economics, April 4, 2025, https://sites.lsa.umich.edu/mje/2025/04/04/algorithmic-trading-and-market-volatility-impact-of-high-frequency-trading/

12. "Algorithmic Trading and Market Volatility: Impact of High-Frequency Trading," Michigan Journal of Economics, April 4, 2025, https://sites.lsa.umich.edu/mje/2025/04/04/algorithmic-trading-and-market-volatility-impact-of-high-frequency-trading/

13. "Feeling queasy about the stock market? Think twice before selling, financial advi-sors say," PBS.org, Aug., 4, 2025, https://www.pbs.org/newshour/economy/feeling-queasy-about-the-stock-market-think-twice-before-selling-financial-advisers-say

14. "6 Steps to Building a Long-Term Investment Strategy," Fidelity Wealth Management, March 7, 2025, https://www.fidelity.com/learning-center/wealth-management-insights/6-steps-to-building-an-investment-strategy

15. "Stocks Whipsaw With S&P 500 on the Precipice of a Bear Market," The New York Times, April 6, 2025, https://www.nytimes.com/2025/04/06/business/stocks-trump-tariff s.html

sell. By educating my clients about historic bear markets and their potential recoveries, I've been able to help reduce that tendency.[16]

Holding those emotions at bay is part of becoming financially educated. If you are financially educated, which it's my job to help you become, you will be less worried about bear markets or even recessions. Education helps you resist emotional decision making and understand that the strategy we've established around your investments is based on your retirement income plan and is designed to help you have a sustainable retirement journey.

RETIREMENT INCOME PLAN AND INVESTMENT STRATEGY AS PROTECTION

Since we've established the importance of consistency, what about protecting you from external events and life changes? The external events that will have an impact on your assets are many, but we've already talked about two of them: recessions and geopolitical turmoil. As I've said, the ideal in retirement planning is to stay as consistent as possible while recalibrating if necessary to adjust for long-term trends.

Another certain external event during retirement is inflation. A projection of 3% inflation per year for 30 years (a long retirement) is a big loss of purchasing power. Our plans include strategies designed to help protect against the impact of inflation.

Life changes in retirement are also very likely to happen. Your health may decline, and either you or your partner will die first, usually. Retirement has a tendency of throwing curveballs like this. But when I get a call from a client saying that they've been diagnosed with cancer, we have an established plan that is designed to help them cope with the financial issues involved in something like this.

We anticipate that there will likely be increased healthcare costs and have baked that into the plan. We don't want you to have to live in

---

16. "How to Define an Investment Strategy," Morningstar, May 5, 2024: https://www. morningstar.com.au/personal-finance/how-to-define-an-investment-strategy.

fear that an upset in the market or in life will throw off your retirement investment strategy. We plan for these events.

DETERMINING YOUR RISK TOLERANCE AND ASSET ALLOCATION

As I've said already, minimizing risk to the assets that provide your retirement income is crucial. Therefore, part of the plan is designed to move assets from high-risk to low-risk investments as you age. The rule of thumb we use here is called the "Rule of 100," and it's pretty simple. While this isn't a guaranteed formula that applies perfectly to everyone, it gives us a good starting point. Let's assume you'll live to age 100—most people won't, obviously, but we do need to plan for the unexpected. The equation is you'll live to age 100 minus your age now equals the percentage of your assets which should be invested in more high-risk investments with potential for growth, like the stock market.

For example, if you're age 62: 100 – 62 = 38. That means at age 62, 38% of your assets should be invested in the stock market versus 62% in low-risk assets. As you age, you can see that more of your assets will be moved into low-risk investments, whereas the proportion of your assets that are high-risk, high-growth potential will decrease, if we're planning correctly.

Lower risk investments include bonds, bond funds and bond exchange-traded funds (ETFs). Precious metals like gold and silver may help diversify your portfolio and hedge against inflation. Another option you may not have considered is life insurance. People look at life insurance as a death benefit, but it may act as a leveraged asset that you can borrow against if there's a need.

Some of my clients have real estate property, like they own an apartment or even an apartment complex which brings in income and should be considered among retirement assets. Even for those who don't, putting money in a Real Estate Investment Trust (REIT) can be a good, low-risk option for many people in or looking at retirement.

CREATING GUARANTEED INCOME FROM YOUR RETIREMENT NEST EGG

Replacing your work paycheck with a retirement income stream means you need sufficient guaranteed income sources. One source of guaranteed income is a fixed index annuity. An annuity, as a reminder, is contract with an insurance company that is designed to generate guaranteed income in retirement for a certain period of years or your lifetime, and potentially your spouse's lifetime as well.[17]

Fixed index annuities provide a guaranteed income benefit that could contribute to your retirement income, in conjunction with other sources of income such as Social Security. Basically, you buy an annuity with a specific lump sum or series of premium payments from an insurance company in exchange for a guaranteed payment when you retire. You can then choose to receive a specific amount of guaranteed income for your lifetime or for a defined time period. Your premium payments are designed to grow in value over the designated accumulation period before you enter retirement.

A fixed index annuity specifically, like other fixed annuity products, protects you against downside risk—that is to say, you can't lose any of the money because of poor market performance on the index it's tied to.[18] Fixed index annuities provide growth potential based on the returns of a specific stock market index tied to your specific annu-ity. You won't get all of the upside, however, with a fixed index annu-ity, your potential interest credits will be based on a participation rate or a cap.[19] The terms of your contract will specify an index and a participation rate. If, for example, over a set period, the index your annuity is tied to goes up 8% and your contract specifies an 80% participation rate, the actual interest you'd get would be 6.4%. A cap on returns specifies in

---

17. "Fixed Indexed and Buffer Annuities Explained," Fidelity Viewpoints, Sept. 23, 2024, https://www.fidelity.com/learning-center/personal-finance/retirement/fixed-indexed-annuity

18. "Fixed Index Annuity Pros and Cons," USAA Life Insurance Co., Aug. 8, 2024, https://www.usaa.com/advice/fixed-index-annuity-pros-and-cons

19. "Fixed Indexed and Buffer Annuities Explained," Fidelity Viewpoints, Sept. 23, 2024, https://www.fidelity.com/learning-center/personal-finance/retirement/fixed-indexed-annuity

advance the percentage you will earn on an FIA during a good market. For example, if you are capped at 5%, then 5% is the most you will ever get in interest.[20] Thus they have the potential for growth, but not all of the upside.[21]

Another feature of FIAs is that most of their fees and costs are built into the product and are not deducted from your annuity value, unless you purchase an additional feature or rider. Surrender fees are charged if you want to get your money out of an annuity before a specific period of time has passed, such as eight to 10 years.[22] Riders are extra enhancements added to your annuity, such as a long-term care rider where the annuity will help pay for certain long-term care expenses if you can no longer perform certain daily activities of living.[23]

There are many fixed index annuities on the market. My goal is to provide the right strategy that aligns with your need for a retirement income, which may include an annuity.

PLANNING FOR LONG-TERM EXPENSES IN RETIREMENT

Ideally you want to both have a retirement income stream and still have enough money for long-term goals. Those are what I talked about in a previous chapter. Many of my clients plan some type of home renovation, will need several new or new-to-them cars during the course of their retirement, and will want to travel. There are many other larger expenses outside of normal day-to-day spending such as car repairs, home repairs, and gifts to children and grandchildren that may need to be taken care of during retirement.

---

20. "Fixed Index Annuity Pros and Cons," USAA Life Insurance Co., Aug. 8, 2024, https://www.usaa.com/advice/fixed-index-annuity-pros-and-cons

21. "Fixed Index Annuity Pros and Cons," USAA Life Insurance Co., Aug. 8, 2024, https://www.usaa.com/advice/fixed-index-annuity-pros-and-cons

22. "How much does an annuity cost? A guide to annuity fees and commissions," Bankrate.com, Aug. 19, 2024, https://www.bankrate.com/retirement/how-much-does-an-annuity-cost/

23. "How much does an annuity cost? A guide to annuity fees and commissions," Bankrate.com, Aug. 19, 2024, https://www.bankrate.com/retirement/how-much-does-an-annuity-cost/

And we can't lose sight of long-term care, which is a cost that must be considered in your retirement income plan. There will likely be other, less expensive healthcare expenses that are still outside of regular healthcare spending, such as hospital and rehabilitation stays that require larger deductibles, and durable medical equipment such as wheelchairs and more.

The goal with this part of your investment strategy is growth and leverage. Investing for growth is intended to, over time, help ensure that the part of your portfolio dedicated to paying for these expenses can grow over time so that you can comfortably pay for vacations, car repairs, gifts to your family, long-term care, and more.

Stocks with all the growth potential may be one component, although as I said above, the percentage of your investments in these should diminish as you age according to the Rule of 100. Direct purchase of stock, stock mutual funds and stock ETFs can all help with this growth portion of your investment strategy, although no investment can ensure a profit and these funds are also subject to losses.

Life insurance, which I also mentioned, is a tool that might also be leveraged during retirement. Some life insurance policies allow you to accumulate cash value that you can then tap for expenses in retirement without paying taxes through policy loans and withdrawals with the option of non-repayment. As we covered earlier in this book, however, excessive distributions could cause the policy to lapse or require additional premiums to keep the policy in force. The loans and withdrawals will reduce the policy's cash value and death benefit.

Many of my clients invest in real estate for their retirement. They may own one or two rental properties that they can either rent out on a monthly basis or a vacation rental on a platform such as VRBO or AirBnB. They might own several apartment buildings that provide a stream of ongoing rental income. You can also invest in a real estate investment trust that provides income.

Precious metals, including gold and silver, are a potential hedge against inflation and can also be source of growth in terms of capital appreciation. My clients appreciate the diversification opportunity offered by precious metals.

IMPORTANCE OF A HOLISTIC INVESTMENT STRATEGY

The holistic investment strategy I've outlined in this chapter and practice with my clients is, in my experience, an effective way to help you seek growth in your portfolio and hence the income in the form of your retirement stream that can help you to have a sustainable retirement as well as meet your legacy goals.

Crafting the right investment strategy for your retirement journey is something I take very seriously. I know that your journey is unique to you and that you need the right investments and products to carry out your plan. I work closely with each and every one of my clients, and their spouses, to help ensure that we get their strategy right and that the products and investments in their portfolios are designed to help provide them with the retirement income, growth potential, inflation protection and sustainability they need to enjoy a long and well-deserved retirement.

UP NEXT

Now that you've gained an understanding of the role of an investment strategy in your retirement income journey, it's time to turn to a crucial component of your retirement income—Social Security. In Chapter 6, we'll explore the nuts and bolts of Social Security so you can understand your options in terms of a claiming strategy that will best serve your unique retirement journey.

6

MAXIMIZING YOUR SOCIAL SECURITY STRATEGY

In my decades of helping people build a sustainable retirement income plan, I've heard just about every mistaken belief about Social Security that's out there. Those misconceptions range is that Social Security is bankrupt, that benefits should be claimed as early as possible, and that individual tax contributions are set aside for individual beneficiaries.[1]

Such misconceptions can lead retirees to make decisions that aren't in alignment with their retirement income journey. For example, if you are fearful about the future of Social Security, you might claim as soon as you turn 62, out of a belief that you should get as much of your benefit as you can in case Social Security isn't here in the future. As you'll learn in this chapter, early claiming permanently reduces your monthly benefit. That doesn't mean you should never claim Social Security at age 62—instead, it means that your claiming decisions should be logical and in line with your unique retirement journey and your retirement income plan.

---

1. "Social Security Financing and Benefits: Myths vs. Facts," U.S. Social Security Administration, Feb. 21, 2024, https://www.ssa.gov/oact/presentations/scgoss_20240221.pdf

When the Trump administration cut jobs at the Social Security Administration in early 2025, many panicked beneficiaries raced to claim their benefits. In fact, new benefit claims were up by more than 15% in March 2025, compared with the same month in 2024.[2] Just like misconceptions, fears based on temporary political moves are usually a mistake.

The complexity of Social Security claiming means that making a claiming mistake is all too easy.

While Social Security Administration employees, and the Social Security website, can provide you with information about your benefits, the claiming process and generic claiming scenarios, they can't give advice regarding your individual claiming strategies.

Paying too much attention to the political chatter about the future of Social Security is typically self-defeating. Barring an economic meltdown of apocalyptic proportions, we'll have Social Security. If not, we have a lot more to worry about. Similarly, it's harmful to make important decisions like when to claim based on what you hear from friends or neighbors. Plus, the older you get, the less you want to be spending the precious time you have left dealing with these ins and outs. Quite simply, you'll likely benefit from professional help to crack this.

That's why it's important to have someone like me along to determine when and how to do it as part of your overall retirement financial strategy. As an independent advisor with the National Social Security Advisor (NSSA®) designation, I offer the knowledge and experience to help my clients identify the right claiming strategy for them. I provide each of my clients with a personalized Social Security Maximization Report, which analyzes factors such as earnings record, life expectancy and finances to calculate when the most beneficial time may be to claim and exactly how much you can expect to receive. This

---

2. "Americans are rushing to claim Social Security Early. Should you?" USA Today, May 1, 2025, https://www.usatoday.com/story/money/2025/04/30/americans-claiming-social-security-early-doge/83340819007/

chapter goes into detail about claiming strategies for couples, single women, people who are still in the workforce, and business owners.

OVERVIEW OF SOCIAL SECURITY BENEFITS

The government calculates your Social Security benefit using your earnings and work history. In 2026, a person earns one Social Security credit for each $1,890 they earn towards a maximum of four credits per year. To be eligible for retirement benefits, you must have at least 40 credits: In other words, means you must have been in the workforce for at least a decade.[3]

The Social Security Administration updates your Social Security statement annually, based on your earnings record. You can access your Social Security statement by creating an account at https://www.ssa.gov/myaccount/. You can check your statement anytime. It's a good idea to look over your statement regularly and verify your earnings amounts to ensure they are correct. You can also use your Social Security account to project your future monthly Social Security benefit using different retirement ages or dates and average future annual salaries if you anticipate raises in the future. You can also compare your benefits as a spouse.

You can claim Social Security between the ages of 62 to 70. The benefit you get increases as you wait to claim, up until age 70 when you've reached your full benefit and there isn't any point in delaying. There are breaks along the path. One important one is age 65, when you become eligible for Medicare. Some people find it beneficial to claim at this age because then their Medicare premium will be automatically deducted from their monthly benefit. And then there is your full retirement age, which differs depending on when you were born. For anyone born in 1960 or later, full retirement age is 67.[4]

---

3. "Latest Amount & QC Explanation," U.S. Social Security Administration, https://www.ssa.gov/oact/cola/QC.html#

4. "Retirement Benefits," U.S. Social Security Administration, 2025, https://www.ssa.gov/pubs/EN-05-10035.pdf

Social Security anchors your benefit on the concept of full retirement age. If you claim earlier than your full retirement age, your benefits are reduced. For example, if you claim at age 62, your benefit would be reduced by approximately 30%. Every year you wait to claim between age 62 and full retirement age of 67, your benefit will increase. Then, if you delay past full retirement age, your benefit will continue to increase until age 70, resulting in a 24% larger benefit.[5]

The following chart is an example of the impact of claiming age on Social Security benefits from the Social Security administration website. Remember, each person's benefit amount will differ and depends on their unique work history, compensation, personal situation, and claiming strategy. I have included this chart to illustrate how claiming at various ages could increase or decrease your benefit amount.

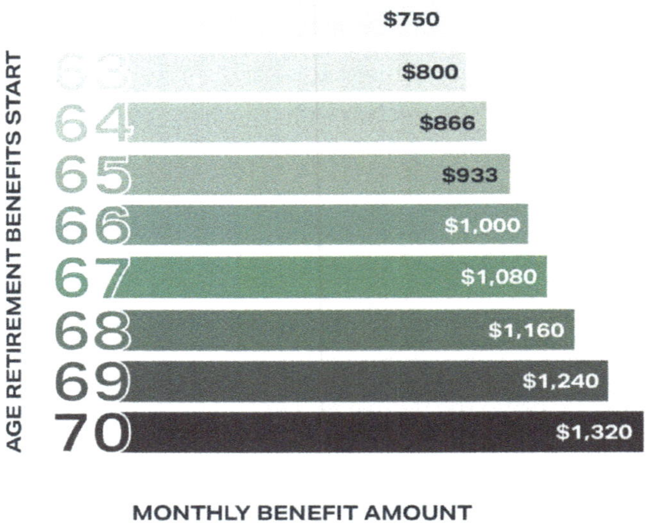

Source: Social Security Administration[6]

5. "Eight Strategies for Deciding When to File for Social Security," Kiplinger, Apr. 16, 2025, https://www.kiplinger.com/retirement/social-security/strategies-for-deciding-when-to-file-for-social-security.

6. "Retirement Ready: Fact Sheet for Workers Ages 61-69," US Social Security Administration, April, 2025, https://www.ssa.gov/myaccount/assets/materials/workers-61-69.pdf

Hypothetical example shown for illustrative purposes only.

Social Security payments are indexed for inflation, meaning that the benefit rises with the cost of living. The cost-of-living adjustment, which is also known as a COLA, is based on inflation as tracked by the Consumer Price Index.[7] The latest COLA was 2.8% for 2026.[8] The fact that your Social Security benefit grows with inflation is extremely important because that's not true of most other sources of income, such as pensions.

You also can't outlive your Social Security—no matter how long you live, you will continue to receive a benefit. As lifespans increase, having a source of income that you can't outlive is incredibly valuable. Life expectancies are variable and unpredictable. However, there are databases available that provide information on how long you are likely to live, on average. According to the life expectancy calculator on the Social Security website, a man born on Jan. 1, 1960, at age 64 and 4 months can expect to live 19 more years for a total life expectancy of 84.4 years.[9] The same life expectancy calculator predicts that a woman born on Jan. 1, 1960 at 64 years and 4 months will live 21.6 more years, until age 87.[10]

It's important to understand that the amount of your benefits is related to your earnings during your working life. Higher earnings mean a higher benefit. Many people top out in earnings as they approach retirement. If you're going to keep working the next couple years with the expectation you'll get annual raises, you might want

---

7. "Social Security's COLA: Let's Not Mess with the Index," Center for Retirement Research at Boston College, Sept. 12, 2024, https://crr.bc.edu/social-securitys-cola-lets-not-mess-with-the-index. Accessed May 23, 2025.

8. "2026 Social Security Changes: Cost-of-Living-Adjustment (COLA), U.S. Social Security Administration, https://www.ssa.gov/news/en/cola/factsheets/2026.html

9. "Retirement and Survivors Benefits: Life Expectancy Calculator," U.S. Social Security Administration, May 26, 2025, https://www.ssa.gov/cgi-bin/longevity.cgi

10. "Retirement and Survivors Benefits: Life Expectancy Calculator," U.S. Social Security Administration, May 26, 2025, https://www.ssa.gov/cgi-bin/longevity.cgi

to delay claiming as increased earnings will have an impact on your ultimate Social Security benefit.

GENERAL SOCIAL SECURITY CLAIMING APPROACHES

In general, if you are in good health and expect to live a long time, it might make sense to wait for a larger monthly benefit, assuming you have sufficient income to meet your needs in the meantime. With some of my clients, when I run their Social Security Maximization report, they find out that it won't make much of a difference to their earnings now by waiting to claim, which gives a nice bit of decision-making room. There are many variables to each client's Social Security situation, which is why there is no one-size-fits-all approach.

There are also good reasons why you might want to claim early, which I'll get to. Right now, I'm telling you to avoid claiming early for silly reasons, like you fear for the future of the program, or this particular decision worked out well for a neighbor, friend or colleague. You can only change your mind once and withdraw your claim so that you can reapply later to increase your benefit amount. That option is only available for one year after you initially claim.[11] After that, you're locked in–you'll have a lower payment forever, over the course of possibly a very long retirement.

Now let's talk about good reasons to consider claiming early. If you have significant health problems, you may want to claim early. You may also have sufficient resources in your savings, so that waiting to claim doesn't make financial sense because you don't need the higher monthly benefit that waiting would provide. Ultimately, it's your money the government is holding onto for you, and you need to be able to access it while you're still alive.

11. "Can I withdraw my Social Security retirement claim and reapply later to increase my benefit amount?" U.S. Social Security Administration, March 13, 2024, https://www.ssa.gov/faqs/en/questions/KA-01993.html

Then of course there are many individuals who have to claim right away at age 62, because they're not in a financial position to wait until their full retirement age at age 67 or 70. Layoffs and downsizing also rarely happen when it's convenient. I have a friend who lost her job during the financial crisis and wasn't able to find another one. After she exhausted many of her financial resources during an extended period of unemployment, she had to claim as soon as she turned age 62.

Then there are others who experience health problem like chronic illnesses such as multiple sclerosis or Parkinson's disease, which may manifest with symptoms that make it difficult, if not impossible to hold the job that they previously held. Others are stricken by cancer and may not be able to work during extended chemotherapy, radiation or immunotherapy treatments or while they are recovering from surgery.

Let's take another hypothetical example of a type of client I deal with frequently. Gerry took four months off his job to recover from a double knee replacement. While he had fully intended to return from work after recovering from his surgeries, he found that he had no appetite to return to the office. He didn't have any physical problems that kept him from working, but a break from the office made him realize that he didn't want to return to an environment that was emotionally and mentally taxing. He came in for an appointment, wondering if it would be possible for him to retire or if he needed to work longer to have a sufficiently large retirement paycheck.

At this point Gerry might confide in me that he just didn't want to face the problematic situations at his office—the gossip, the back-biting and rumors. Being at home in a restful environment away from the day-to-day environment at work would have made him realize how uncomfortable the work environment was so, if at all possible, he was ready to put in his retirement papers and never go back to work again. In this case, if the numbers added up, I might be able to tell him that he could retire without putting any more time in at work.

For some people, delaying claiming by a year or two, like in the situation I just described, doesn't make that much of a difference. It is very interesting to see how many people think they want to work longer, even for several years, but once they find out they have a strategy that allows them to retire sooner, they do.

WORKING WHILE CLAIMING SOCIAL SECURITY

You can claim Social Security and continue to work. Whether you should do so is a different question. For some people it's the right approach. They still have goals they want to accomplish in their career or feel better with the work schedule. Income from both the job and Social Security may enable you to enjoy a needed standard of living.

And again, because many wage-earners are at their maximum earnings potential as they approach retirement, and your benefit is based on your average monthly wage during your highest 35 years of employment, working longer than 35 years can boost your monthly benefit.[12] But whether you want to and are capable of continuing work can't be your only consideration, unfortunately. That's because if you claim Social Security before full retirement age, you are subject to an earnings limitation if you want to be able to collect your full benefit. If you exceed these earning limits, you will have to give back $1 for every $2 you earn above this limit. In 2026, the earnings limit was $24,480.[13] Every $2 you earn above this limit will mean $1 less in your benefit. This figure includes wages, bonuses, commissions, and vacation pay, but not pensions, annuities, investment income, interest, veteran's or other government benefits.[14]

In the year that you reach full retirement age, the earnings limit rises. In 2026, that limit was $65,160 in the months before you reach

---

12. "Plan to Work and Claim Social Security? 2 Pros and 3 Cons to Weigh First," The Motley Fool, Mar. 15, 2025: https://www.fool.com/retirement/2025/03/15/working-and-claiming-social-security-pros-and-cons

13. ""2026 Social Security Changes: Cost-of-Living-Adjustment (COLA), U.S. Social Security Administration, https://www.ssa.gov/news/en/cola/factsheets/2026.html

14. "What happens if I work and get Social Security retirement benefits?" U.S. Social Security Administration, Jan. 2, 2025, https://www.ssa.gov/faqs/en/questions/KA-01921.html

your full retirement age. During that year, $1 in benefits will be deducted for every $3 you earn above that limit.[15] As you continue to work, you will continue to pay Social Security taxes on your earning, which may increase your monthly benefit.[16] Once you reach your full retirement age, you will receive your benefits with no limit on your earnings. And once you reach full retirement age, your benefits will be recalculated to reflect any funds withheld from your benefits while you were working.

CLAIMING STRATEGIES FOR COUPLES

When you are married, there are many Social Security claiming strategies. That's why understanding all your options is so helpful, which is what the Social Security Maximization Report provides. Because many married couples have significant earning differences, and women are more likely to outlive their husbands, you need to be educated about all the potential options out there.

Before getting into the nuances of claiming strategies for couples, you should understand some basic facts about Social Security benefits when a spouse is involved. Social Security spousal benefits often make sense for spouses who earn a significantly lower amount than their spouse. You need to evaluate whether claiming 100% of your Social Security would be more beneficial than claiming 50% of your spouse's benefit.[17] If you've been a stay-at-home parent or spouse, you may not have enough credits to claim Social Security on your own. In that case, spousal benefits are your only option. Spousal benefits also max out at

---

15. "What happens if I work and get Social Security retirement benefits?" U.S. Social Security Administration, Jan. 2, 2025, https://www.ssa.gov/faqs/en/questions/KA-01921.html

16. "What happens if I work and get Social Security retirement benefits?" U.S. Social Security Administration, Jan. 2, 2025, https://www.ssa.gov/faqs/en/questions/KA-01921.html

17. "Do you qualify for Social Security Spouse's benefits?" U.S. Social Security Administration, April 18, 2025, https://blog.ssa.gov/do-you-qualify-for-social-security-spouses-benefits-2/

full retirement age. In other words, a spousal benefit doesn't increase past full retirement age.[18]

Some of the basics of spousal benefits are:[19]

- You must be at least age 62 to claim them and you and your partner must have been married for at least a year.
- You can't collect spousal benefits unless your spouse is already receiving Social Security.
- If you claim at age 62, when you are initially eligible, you can receive a reduced benefit of your partner's benefit at their full retirement age. If your spouse claims Social Security before his full retirement age, your benefit will be reduced. Like your own benefit, this percentage increases in steps depending on the year you were born until you reach your own full retirement age.

By this point, you're realizing that while being married increases your options and can be beneficial for your retirement plan in general, to get the real advantage means weighing a number of variables including you and your partner's age, life expectancy, health and timetable to retire.

Let's look at a hypothetical situation to see what different options exist for claiming for a married couple, who we will call Joe and Maura. At the beginning of 2025, when I was writing this chapter, Joe was age 62 and Maura was age 61. Their retirement ages are 67 and a total income need per year is $70,000. Maura worked part time for many years, and while she does have enough credits to claim her own benefit, Joe has a significantly larger benefit. The goal of a Social Security maximization strategy is to determine the largest benefit available over a lifetime for Joe and Maura, adding up the monthly benefit to calculate a total over their expected lifespan. The projection we'll use for this example shows Joe passing away at age 81 and Maura passing away at age 84.

---

18. "Do you qualify for Social Security Spouse's benefits?" U.S. Social Security Administration, April 18, 2025, https://blog.ssa.gov/do-you-qualify-for-social-security-spouses-benefits-2/

19. "Do you qualify for Social Security Spouse's benefits?" U.S. Social Security Administration, April 18, 2025, https://blog.ssa.gov/do-you-qualify-for-social-security-spouses-benefits-2/

With a couple, I want to maximize the surviving spouse's benefit so that, along with the rest of their retirement income plan, Maura doesn't experience a significant reduction in her living standard when Joe passes away. Single people have many of the same expenses as married couples do in retirement—they need a place to live, a car, food, heat, air conditioning and so on. For Maura to experience a significant reduction in her living standard at age 80 would be extremely difficult, and this isn't anything that either of them wants to see happen. By producing a report on their optimal Social Security Strategy, I can help them understand their options and build a plan that helps them maintain the lifestyle they want throughout their retirement.

A personalized analysis, based on the proprietary Social Security Timing® report revealed that a Social Security strategy that involved Joe filing for his monthly benefit at age 68 and five months would yield an approximate benefit of $4,552. At age 67, Maura will begin receiving a benefit. Over their lifetimes, Maura and Joe would receive a lifetime family benefit of $833,438.

When Joe passes away, then, Maura would receive his benefit, which at that point would have increased in value due to the yearly cost-of-living adjustment, which I described earlier in the chapter. With their other resources, Maura would be better positioned and able to maintain her standard of living for the rest of her life.

Spousal Benefits for the Divorced: Spousal benefits are also available for divorced spouses if the marriage lasted at least 10 years and you've been divorced for at least two years.[20] Those benefits don't affect your former spouse's benefit. Divorced spousal benefits are 50% of your former spouse's Social Security benefit.[21] If you remarry, you

---

20. "Divorced Spouses Maximize Social Security Benefits by Navigating some Tricky Rules," Forbes.com, Feb. 24, 2024, https://www.forbes.com/sites/bobcarlson/2024/02/24/divorced-spouses-maximize-social-security-benefits-by-navigating-some-tricky-rules/

21. "Divorced Spouses Maximize Social Security Benefits by Navigating some Tricky Rules," Forbes.com, Feb. 24, 2024, https://www.forbes.com/sites/bobcarlson/2024/02/24/divorced-spouses-maximize-social-security-benefits-by-navigating-some-tricky-rules/

lose access to your former spouse's benefit. However, if your former spouse dies, you then become eligible for full survivor's benefits, which is 100% of their benefit.[22]

Spousal Benefits for Widows: Spousal benefits are available for widowed spouses, provided the marriage lasted for one year.[23] If your spouse dies, you are eligible for full survivor's benefits, based on 100% of their Social Security.

CLAIMING STRATEGIES FOR INDEPENDENT WOMEN

For independent women, the decisions around when to claim Social Security are more straightforward than for couples. That's because there is only one benefit in question. I work with many independent women who aren't married. I also work with others who are divorced or widowed.

In general, women are more reliant on Social Security benefits than men. They both tend to earn less and live longer on average. Among beneficiaries who are age 65 and older, 44% of women receive at least half of their income from Social Security, as opposed to 39% of male beneficiaries.[24] What single women receive is dependent on factors like widowhood, divorce, their own history of employment, their wages during their employed years and when they claim.[25]

---

22. "Social Security Benefits After Divorce: In some cases 'your ex is worth twice as much dead than alive,' expert says," CNBC.com, March 19, 2024, https://www.cnbc. com/2024/03/19/how-social-security-benefits-change-after-divorce-death.html

23. "How does Social Security work when a spouse dies?" AARP.org, March 31, 2025, https://www.aarp.org/social-security/faq/when-spouse-dies/

24. "Social Security Eligibility for Women: Claiming Strategies and Eligibility Explained," The Street, Mar. 11, 2025 https://www.thestreet.com/retirement-daily/social-security-medicare/social-security-for-women-claiming-strategies-eligibility-explained-

25. "Social Security Eligibility for Women: Claiming Strategies and Eligibility Explained," The Street, Mar. 11, 2025 https://www.thestreet.com/retirement-daily/social-security-medicare/social-security-for-women-claiming-strategies-eligibility-explained-

Let's look at a Social Security optimization report for a hypothetical client we will call Susan. Susan was born in 1971, which makes her 54 at the beginning of 2025. If Susan claimed at the earliest possible point in time, at age 62, she would receive a monthly benefit of $2,330. If she waited until age 70, her benefit would be $4,960 a month.

When maximizing Social Security, it is important to consider what I call the "break-even point." Understanding the break-even point is crucial when balancing the risks of claiming early and missing out on a longer monthly payment versus the risks of claiming later and dying soon after you claim, missing out on getting as much out of your benefit as you could have if you had claimed earlier.[26]

The report I might run for Susan notes that her break-even point is at age 81. Using that number, as well as a life expectancy of 83 years, I might suggest that Susan claim her benefits at age 66, when she would receive a monthly benefit of approximately $3,385. Using this strategy, her expected lifetime benefit would be a total of $332,570. Claiming as early as possible, at age 62 and 1 month, would reduce her monthly benefit to $2,330, with a total expected lifetime benefit of $322,191.

Because we assume that Susan will live until age 83, it might make sense for her to wait until age 66 to claim Social Security so that she would receive a larger benefit for the remaining 17 years of her life.

CLAIMING STRATEGIES FOR BUSINESS OWNERS

If you are self-employed or own a business, you earn Social Security credits the same way as employees do: $1,890 in earnings equals one credit for up to four credits per year of earnings.[27] The only difference

26. "Social Security break-even point: What it is and how to calculate yours," Thrivent.-com, Dec. 19, 2024, https://www.thrivent.com/insights/social-security/social-security-break-even-point-what-it-is-how-to-calculate-yours

27. "How You Earn Credits," Social Security Administration, 2025, https://www.ssa.gov/ pubs/EN-05-10072.pdf

between wage-earners and the self-employed/business owners when it comes to Social Security is that if you're the latter, net earnings are used to calculate your benefit, whereas things like bonuses and commissions can come into play for employees.

Many business owners I work with have sought to minimize taxes by reducing their income. To achieve this goal, they may form a limited liability company or LLC and file their taxes as a Subchapter S Corporation. Then they can pay themselves a wage through a W-2 and receive other income from their business in the form of distributions, which aren't subject to Social Security tax. Of course, they must pay themselves a fair wage. Still, reducing the amount of their income subject to Social Security tax will reduce the amount of Social Security that they receive in the future.

This is something we have to look at when we create their retirement income plan. If there is less coming from Social Security, there needs to be more coming from other sources such as retirement savings, rental properties, side jobs or consulting. If I'm working with someone who is five or more years away from retirement, they can potentially adjust the amount they are paying themselves to increase their eventual Social Security benefit. If they are close to retirement, that may not be worthwhile or possible.

UP NEXT

Since Social Security is a key source of income in retirement for most Americans, except perhaps the extraordinarily wealthy, it's important to take the decision of when and how to claim your benefits seriously as part of your retirement financial strategy. The decision, like when you choose to retire, is typically permanent and can't be reversed. You don't want to be in your late 80s or early 90s trying to make ends meet with your $700 check and wondering why on earth you claimed Social Security at age 62.

Now that you understand the importance of finding the most appropriate Social Security claiming strategy, in Chapter 7 we move on to another critical topic, building a tax strategy. I always say that it isn't what you have, it's what you keep. In the next chapter you'll learn about the strategies to help minimize the amount of taxes you pay in retirement.

7

HOW TO GET THE GOVERNMENT OUT OF YOUR POCKET

Many couples and individuals preparing for retirement expect to pay less in taxes after settling into their new life as a retiree, but there is no guarantee that this will happen unless you engage in careful retirement income planning.

Despite current legislative trends, there is a good chance that tax rates will rise in the future. There is also the possibility that tax laws will change, which could scramble the tax planning that you engaged in before retirement. Regardless of what's happening with tax policy and politics, the important thing to remember is that there is no way to avoid paying taxes. Since you must pay taxes, it makes sense to plan accordingly because the more you pay in taxes the less you will have available to spend on making the most of your golden years.

Consider a case of this type of client. We'll call them Dave and Susan. They are diligent savers and have many questions and some assumptions about retirement that weren't factually grounded. Because most of their savings was in the form of qualified retirement funds in 401(k)-type accounts, and some other factors that this chapter will explore, their tax bill was likely to rise in retirement in the absence of a tax mitigation plan. They were surprised to find out that taxes could cut more deeply into their savings—and their retirement income—to a greater extent than they had realized. I'll share more about their story, and the story of other hypothetical clients, in this chapter.

That means you want to engage in proactive planning so you can help mitigate the impact that taxes will have on your income and assets during a retirement retirement (extended unemployment) could last 25 to 30 years. Such planning can help you maximize your income and your assets during your extended period of unemployment. In this chapter, we will discuss strategies to help do just that, beginning with an overview of the types of taxes that each retiree will owe during retirement, then covering the unexpected tax burdens retirees may face, followed by key tax mitigation strategies, and culminating in an in-depth discussion of how we help our clients approach this primary directive.

WHAT KINDS OF TAXES WILL YOU OWE IN RETIREMENT

The kinds of taxes for retirees are essentially stable from work life moving into retirement. The first set is comprised of the income taxes. The main component is the federal income tax, which can be mitigated but not avoided. As this chapter will illustrate, in retirement the sources of income that are subject to tax typically include traditional retirement accounts such as traditional 401(k)s and IRAs, Social Security, pensions, rental property income, capital gains, market-based investments, and certain types of insurance income from annuities and permanent life insurance policies.

When you reach age 65 and claim Medicare, you may be subject to higher Medicare premiums if your income is above certain thresholds. In 2026, higher Medicare premiums for Medicare Parts B and D begin for single filers and married people filing separately at $109,000 and for joint filers over $218,000 of modified adjusted gross income,[1] In

1. "2026 Medicare Parts A&B Premiums and Deductibles," U.S. Centers for Medicare and Medicaid, Nov. 14, 2025, https://www.cms.gov/newsroom/fact-sheets/2026-medicare-parts-b-

other words, the premium surcharges are based on your modified adjusted gross income from the tax year two years ago because the Social Security Administration determines surcharge eligibility based on the income you reported two years ago.[2] More on this later in the chapter.

The second tax is state income tax, which is wildly variable depending on the state of residence. Of the 50 states in America, 42 states levy some kind of income tax.[3] Of those states, only one—Washington—does not include a tax on income from wages and salary.[4] Washington does tax capital gains income.[5] The other 41 states can be separated further into those with a flat tax rate across all income brackets and those with two or more brackets.[6] Fourteen states fall into the former category, and the remaining 27 have top marginal tax rates ranging from 2.5% all the way up to 14.4% in California.[7]

---

premiums-deductibles

2. "Medicare Premiums 2025: IRMAA Brackets and Surcharges for Parts B and D," Kipliner.com, May 7, 2025, https://www.kiplinger.com/retirement/medicare/medicare-premiums-2025-irmaa-for-parts-b-and-d

3. "State Individual Income Tax Rates and Brackets, 2025," Tax Foundation, Feb. 18, 2025, https://taxfoundation.org/data/all/state/state-income-tax-rates/

4. "State Individual Income Tax Rates and Brackets, 2025," Tax Foundation, Feb. 18, 2025, https://taxfoundation.org/data/all/state/state-income-tax-rates/

5. "State Individual Income Tax Rates and Brackets, 2025," Tax Foundation, Feb. 18, 2025, https://taxfoundation.org/data/all/state/state-income-tax-rates/

6. "State Individual Income Tax Rates and Brackets, 2025," Tax Foundation, Feb. 18, 2025, https://taxfoundation.org/data/all/state/state-income-tax-rates/

7. "State Individual Income Tax Rates and Brackets, 2025," Tax Foundation, Feb. 18, 2025, https://taxfoundation.org/data/all/state/state-income-tax-rates/

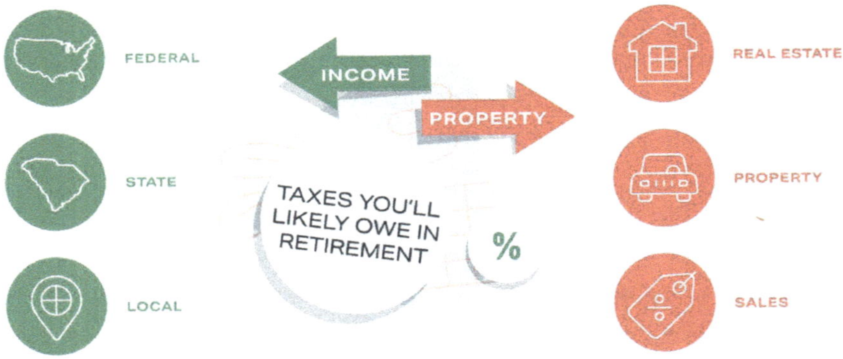

Some retirees consider moving to states with no income tax when they retire to save the money that they would have otherwise spent on state income tax. However, the actual savings from a move like this isn't always as much as you might think. That's because states with no income tax rely on other types of taxes for revenue, which can cost you as much, or even more, than what you might have spent on state income taxes. Tennessee, for example, is a favored retirement destination due to its mild climate and lack of state income tax. However, the Tax Foundation reports that Tennessee's combined state and average sales tax rate of 9.56% ranks as the second highest of all states.[8]

After the income taxes, the other category is property tax, all of which will be imposed by the state or county where the property is owned or registered. The bulk of this tax is usually comprised of the property tax on any real estate owned by the retiree, including homes, apartments and condominiums whether they are a primary domicile, vacation property or owned for the purpose of deriving rental income. As home prices have risen, property taxes have risen in tandem. For homeowners on a fixed retirement income, property tax increases can negatively impact their budget. Consider metro Phoenix, another popular destination for retirees, where property taxes in Maricopa

8. "State and Local Sales Tax Rates, 2025," Feb. 4, 2025, https://taxfoundation.org/data/ all/state/sales-tax-rates/

County have risen by 15.4% since 2019 as home prices surged by 64.3%.[9] In South Carolina, another favored retiree locale, property taxes have risen on average by 28.6% since the pandemic or 5.7% a year.

The second item in the category is tax on vehicles. Both items are also variable depending on state of residence or location of property. More than half of the states in the country levy personal property taxes on vehicles, and the range of vehicles is usually quite broad and can include even utility vehicles and some kinds of trailers.[10]

These examples of the impact of state sales, property and income tax illustrate that when it comes to retirement income planning, you should plan holistically. That means considering what your overall income and spending power will look like in retirement based on your retirement income plan, rather than analyzing factors like income tax in isolation.

HOW TAXES CHANGE IN RETIREMENT

The main issue for many retirees is that their tax burden becomes reconfigured in unexpected ways during retirement. The primary portion that makes up the bulk of taxes a retiree will owe is usually attributable to income, and this is where most of the post-retirement variance occurs as well.

The first thing that many retirees have a difficult time planning for is a loss of tax deductions in retirement. A scrupulous accountant or even a thoughtful individual can significantly reduce their tax burdens in the working years by maximizing the deductions they claim on their income tax.

Unfortunately, most of those disappear in or around the first years of retirement. Many retirees end up having to switch from a specific, highly itemized set of deductions to the standard deduction. One

---

9. "2024 property tax balloon causing sticker shock for homeowners," Cotality.com, Jan. 8, 2025, https://www.cotality.com/insights/articles/why-did-property-taxes-go-up-2024

10. "Missouri and Kansas have some of the highest property taxes on vehicles in the country," Kansas City Star, March 8, 2024, https://www.kansascity.com/news/local/article286402800.html

factor that influences this is the presence or absence of a mortgage, as many retirees have either already paid off their mortgage or plan to finish paying off their mortgage before they retire. For people like Dave and Susan (remember they're a type rather than real clients), who had paid off their mortgage several years ago, the realization that a lack of itemized deductions might hurt even more in retirement could be an unpleasant surprise.

When the mortgage has not been paid off before retirement, we have a process to help you determine whether this would be the right decision or not. If the interest on the money owed for the house is higher than the interest that is being received for investments, that might signal that the mortgage could be paid off before retirement, otherwise we risk the money owed on the mortgage cutting into income. Setting up the right approach to taxes in retirement can make a big difference between thriving and scraping by. Much of the tax burden in retirement comes not from changes in deductions, but the variable sources of income that retirees most often seek to draw upon.

Any tax-deferred account such as a 401(k) requires the retiree to begin to take a yearly required minimum distribution (RMD) by age 73 or 75, depending on the year of birth.[11] Anyone born in 1959 or later has an RMD of age 75, according to the SECURE Act 2.0.[12] The gradual delay of RMDs from age 70-and-a-half gives you more time to plan, and also for your accounts to compound. But unless you plan, if you wait to pull distributions from your qualified retirement accounts until you are age 75, those distributions will be larger, which will mean paying more in taxes. That's because RMD calculations are based on IRS life expectancy so the later you start RMDs, the higher they will be.[13]

---

11. "Required Minimum Distribution (RMD) Rules for Original Owners of Retirement Accounts," Congress.gov, Aug. 29, 2024, https://www.congress.gov/crs-product/IF12750

12. "Required Minimum Distribution (RMD) Rules for Original Owners of Retirement Accounts," Congress.gov, Aug. 29, 2024, https://www.congress.gov/crs-product/IF12750

13. "Publication 590-B – Introductory Material," US Internal Revenue Service, March 20, 2025, https://www.irs.gov/publications/p590b#en_US_2024_publink100090310

For Dave and Susan, if they began taking distributions from their $1.5 million in joint traditional IRAs at age 72, their joint RMD would be $54,744.53. Waiting until age 75 would mean an RMD of $60,975.61. As they age, their RMD will continue to increase because their life expectancy grows shorter over time. Let's say at age 80 they have joint traditional IRAs worth $1.25 million. In that case, their RMD would be $61,8881.82.

Also, if the value of their traditional IRA rises due to an increase in stock or bond prices or the additions of interest or dividends, their RMDs will also increase. If instead of a $1.25 million IRA at age 80, their joint traditional IRA was worth $1.5 million due to stock price appreciation, for example, their RMD would be $74,257.43. Of course, asset appreciation is a good thing—but it does typically come with higher taxes. Also, since traditional IRAs are taxed at ordinary income tax rates, you don't benefit from lower capital tax rates when you withdraw money in retirement.[14]

While the assets of 401(k) and IRAs are gaining in popularity and the pension as a source of income in retirement is increasingly rare, for a variety of state and government employees pensions can end up representing a significant amount of their overall income for retirement. Because pension contributions are made on a tax-deferred basis, when they are withdrawn, they will be subject to income tax. In fact, like traditional IRAs, pensions are taxed at ordinary income rates.[15] Social Security payments are also subject to your federal marginal income tax rate, although this does not apply to 100% of income from Social Security. It will apply to either zero, half of your Social Security benefit or 85%, depending on your situation. Nine states tax Social Security benefits—Colorado, Connecticut, Minnesota, Montana, New Mexico,

---

14. "IRA Taxes: Contributions, Withdrawals and More," Thrivent.com, Feb. 12, 2025, https://www.thrivent.com/insights/taxes/ira-taxes-contributions-withdrawals-more

15. "How the IRS Taxes Retirement Income," Kiplinger.com, Nov. 13, 2024, https://www. kiplinger.com/taxes/how-retirement-income-is-taxed

Rhode Island, Utah, Vermont and West Virginia—although many offset those taxes with credits and discounts.[16]

The third aspect of retirement that makes the tax situation more challenging are the new taxes that pre-retirees are not subjected to, as well as the potential for changes to the tax code that can increase tax rates or decrease the available tax mitigation strategies. One common tax that many retirees do not see coming is Medicare tax, as I mentioned earlier. Many people planning retirement do not understand that although Medicare can help some individuals lower their healthcare costs, it is by no means free and depending on the individual's situation may increase their costs associated with health insurance by a significant margin.

Medicare costs are dictated by the Social Security Act, and include premiums, deductibles and coinsurance payments. Even to those who are aware of these fees, it may be easy to discount their presence until the reality sets in, when a few hundred dollars a month in income can be the difference between breezing through retirement and a struggle to maintain your desired quality of life. Specifically, the Medicare premiums that I mentioned earlier are tied to your modified adjusted gross income from two years ago, which means that the more taxable income you have, the more potential you have for higher Medicare premiums.

Here's an example of how that might work. Consider the hypothetical clients Steve and Katie, a married couple who live in Simpsonville, South Carolina. Steve is a very successful engineer at the BMW Plant in Spartanburg. Katie worked part time as a teacher's aide in public middle schools, but retired several years ago. Based on their retirement savings in a 401(k) account, a pension that Steve will receive from BMW, rental property income, and their estimated Social Security, their modified adjusted gross income will translate into a Medicare premium surcharge of $185 a month for each of them, on top

---

16. "States that Tax Social Security Benefits in 2025," Kiplinger.com, June 22, 2025, https://www.kiplinger.com/retirement/social-security/603803/states-that-tax-social-security-benefits

of their regular monthly premium of $185 each, which adds up to $370 a month or $4,440 a year.[17] However, there are a number of strategies we might employ to assist with tax mitigation to help reduce their modified adjusted gross income and potentially have no premium surcharge. In this situation, they could pay the basic monthly Medicare premium of $185 a month, which is usually deducted from Social Security.

POTENTIAL FOR FEDERAL RATES TO RISE IN THE FUTURE

One significant issue, which is ultimately unpredictable, is the likelihood that taxes will rise at some point in the future, according to experts who view the federal budget deficit and overall federal debt as unsustainable.[18] As of October 2025, the federal budget deficit was $486 billion; cumulatively, the fiscal year 2025 deficit was $1.78 trillion.[19,20] The debt represents the total amount of money the federal government owes, while the deficit is the difference between what the government takes in for revenue and spends on expenses.[21] The federal debt is the accumulated deficits that have occurred in the past, minus any surpluses.[22] Over time, the federal budget deficit has increased because expenses are higher than revenue.[23]

---

17. "2025 Medicare Parts A & B Premiums and Deductibles," US Centers for Medicaid and Medicare, Nov. 8, 2024, https://www.cms.gov/newsroom/fact-sheets/2025-medicare-parts-b-premiums-and-deductibles

18. "Sustaining U.S. Government Debt Will Force Hard Choices in the Future," TD Bank, June 5, 2024, https://economics.td.com/us-debt-sustainability

19. "US Hits $38 Trillion in Debt, After the Fastest Accumulation of $1 Trillion Outside Pandemic," PBS, Oct. 23, 2025: https://www.pbs.org/newshour/politics/u-s-hits-38-trillion-in-debt-after-the-fastest-accumulation-of-1-trillion-outside-of-the-pandemic

20. "What Is the National Deficit?" "U.S. Department of the Treasury, https://fiscaldata. treasury. gov/americas-finance-guide/national-deficit.

21. "Debt vs. Deficits: What's the Difference?" Peter G. Peterson Foundation, April 16, 2025, https://www.pgpf.org/article/debt-vs-deficits-whats-the-difference/

22. Debt vs. Deficits: What's the Difference?" Peter G. Peterson Foundation, April 16, 2025, https://www.pgpf.org/article/debt-vs-deficits-whats-the-difference/

23. "Debt vs. Deficits: What's the Difference?" Peter G. Peterson Foundation, April 16, 2025, https://www.pgpf.org/article/debt-vs-deficits-whats-the-difference/

Many candidates have run on a platform of fiscal responsibility by reducing government spending. This will remain the likely focus of most legislation aimed at reducing the deficit. One other way to reduce the deficit is through increasing taxes. While raising income tax rates wasn't on the table with President Trump's One Big Beautiful Bill Act in 2025, such tax increases could happen in the future—we just don't know how, when, or if that will happen.[24] This is why tax planning is important, so that you have strategies to cope with different potential economic events that might affect you in the future.

TAX MITIGATION STRATEGIES IN RETIREMENT: ROTH CONVERSIONS

Luckily, there are many strategies we deploy to help mitigate the tax burden on our clients. One way to do this is through conversion from 401(k) or Traditional IRAs into a Roth IRA[25]. There are no silver bullets when it comes to tax, but if used thoughtfully, the conversion can make a significant difference. Since Roth funds are withdrawn tax-free (after age 59-1/2 and the account has been open for at least 5 years), the tax has to be paid up front. According to Fidelity's Roth IRA conversion calculator, if you wanted to convert $100,000 and you were currently in a 27.8% federal tax bracket and a 5% state tax bracket, the tax due on conversion would be $32,800.[26]

Ideally, for a conversion to make sense financially, you should pay the taxes due on the conversion from current savings or income. There are also strategies you can employ that can reduce the potential bill.

---

24. "H.R. 1 – One Big Beautiful Bill Act," 119th Congress (2025 -2026), June 27, 2025, https://www.congress.gov/bill/119th-congress/house-bill/1/text

25. Converting an employer plan account to a Roth IRA is a taxable event. Increased taxable income from the Roth IRA conversion may have several consequences including (but not limited to) a need for additional tax withholding or estimated tax payments, the loss of certain tax deductions and credits, and higher taxes on Social Security benefits and higher Medicare premiums. Be sure to consult with a qualified tax advisor before making any decisions regarding your IRA.

26. Roth IRA Conversion Calculator, Fidelity: https://www.fidelity.com/calculators-tools/roth-conversion-calculator.

For example, you could retire and live on savings for a year plus a small amount of income that would keep you in the 10 or 12% tax bracket and convert in that year, when your tax bracket would be lower than normal, allowing you to pay less tax. But by paying the tax now and letting the investment grow, that increase in tax-free income later can provide you with financial flexibility that can help you move forward on your retirement journey.

One of the major benefits of a Roth conversion is that it is not subject to the rules of RMD like a Traditional IRA, meaning that if your retirement income is taken care of through other sources, you can leave your Roth account alone and let the account potentially grow unhindered as a way of increasing the amount of money in your estate. The other way to fund a Roth outside of conversions is simply through yearly contributions via regular work income, and since that income arrives having already been taxed, it goes in without further need to pay additional tax. These contributions into the Roth account have to be in the account a minimum of five years to be considered tax-free funds. However, Roth contributions are subject to income limitations. If you file as an individual or head of household, you can make up to $150,000 and make a $7,500 contribution if you are under age 50 or an $8,600 contribution if you are age 50 or over, the maximum allowed, to a Roth IRA.[27] Your ability to contribute to a Roth gradually phases out between $150,000 and $164,999 for a single person and between $236,000 and $246,000 for a married couple filing jointly.[28] When you hit an income of $165,000 or more for a single person and $236,000 or more for a married couple filing jointly, you make too much money to contribute.[29]

---

27. "Roth IRA Contribution Limits for 2025 and 2026," Fidelity.com, Nov. 13, 2025, https://www.fidelity.com/learning-center/smart-money/roth-ira-contribution-limits

28. "Roth IRA Contribution Limits for 2025 and 2026," Fidelity.com, Nov. 13, 2025, https://www.fidelity.com/learning-center/smart-money/roth-ira-contribution-limits

29. "Roth IRA Contribution Limits for 2025 and 2026," Fidelity.com, Nov. 13, 2025, https://www.fidelity.com/learning-center/smart-money/roth-ira-contribution-limits

TAX MITIGATION STRATEGIES IN RETIREMENT: INSURANCE

One other avenue to mitigate taxation in retirement and estate planning is through the purchase of a life insurance policy. This tool is often misunderstood and underutilized, because its name makes it seem deceptively straightforward as only a tool to pay out a benefit for heirs in the event of the policyholder's death. And that is true, that is the primary purpose.

However, there are two main kinds of life insurance policies, and the less common one provides an additional amount of flexibility. Most people tend to be familiar with term life insurance policies, which are primarily used to insure against the death of a bread-winner with a family. The second category is a permanent life insurance policy. And while its primary purpose is also to provide a death benefit to your loved ones, it can accumulate cash value within it, which can be used to withdraw funds during retirement or borrow against. This retirement concept is often utilized by business owners if there was not an opportunity to contribute to a 401(k) or employer sponsor-funded program. Parents and grandparents might also utilize this concept to fund and build tax-free funds for their children and grandchildren.

When a retiree withdraws from their permanent life insurance policy, they will be allowed to withdraw a defined portion of the policy's cash value or their premium payments without paying taxes, assuming the policy is not considered a "Modified Endowment Contract," or MEC. So, if the total premiums paid into the policy are

$300,000 and the policy has generated $40,000 in interest accumulation for a total value of $340,000 the retiree might be able to withdraw up to $300,000 before being subject to taxes on the withdrawal.

The other way in which permanent policies differ from term policies is the ability to borrow against the policy. Retirees with a permanent life insurance policy may, depending on the terms, borrow up to 90% of the total value of the policy's cash value without paying taxes. Repayment is often optional. If you choose to repay you are paying yourself back on this variety of loan. If you choose not to repay the loan, the amount will be deducted from the death benefit. The sweet spot in this tax-free strategy is the policy typically continues to compound interest as if the funds borrowed are still in the account. It's crucial to note, however, that excessive withdrawals or loans could cause the policy to lapse or require additional premiums to keep the policy in force.

TAX MITIGATION STRATEGIES IN RETIREMENT: FIXED INCOME ANNUITIES

Another type of asset that can help to mitigate taxes is the fixed income annuity. As discussed in earlier chapters, fixed index annuities offer the opportunity for ongoing income and also ensure that your annuity cannot lose money due to market losses. Non-qualified annuities are also not subject to contribution limits associated with other retirement savings vehicles, such as IRAs and 401(k)s. If you hold an annuity within a qualified plan, however, such as an IRA, you will have the same contribution limits applied.

A fixed income annuity can be funded with money that has or has not been taxed. You can use a pretax account, such as an IRA or a 401(k) to hold an annuity. You can also purchase an annuity with after-tax dollars outside of a retirement account. When you earn interest on an annuity, whether it is inside or outside a retirement savings account, you don't have to pay any taxes on that interest until you decide to withdraw it.[30]

If you hold an annuity within a qualified retirement account, that annuity will be subject to RMD rules when you turn either age 73 or 75, depending on how old you are.[31] If, on the other hand, you own an annuity outside of a retirement account, that annuity is not subject to

---

30. "How Are Annuity Withdrawals Taxed?" Kiplinger.com, Oct. 28, 2024, https://www.kiplinger.com/retirement/annuities/602248/how-annuities-are-taxed

31. "How is an Annuity Taxed?" Northwestern Mutual, Feb. 28, 2025, https://www.northwesternmutual.com/life-and-money/how-is-an-annuity-taxed/

RMD rules, which means you can let that account grow and defer taxes until you decide you want to withdraw funds from it.[32] If you withdraw money from any kind of a deferred annuity, that income will be taxed as ordinary income rather than capital gains income.

Because withdrawals from annuities held outside of a retirement account include the principal you used to purchase the annuity in the first plan, only the interest portion of the annuity is taxable.[33] If you own an annuity, you must wait until you turn 59-1/2 to withdraw money, otherwise you will pay a 10% penalty on the interest earnings you've withdrawn, plus ordinary income tax.[34] One interesting tax wrinkle with annuities is that annuity interest that is used to pay long-term care insurance premiums or for long-term care can typically be withdrawn tax-free.[35]

TAX MITIGATION STRATEGIES: HEALTH SAVINGS ACCOUNTS

The last significant strategy we will discuss here to help lower your tax liability is the Healthcare Savings Account (HSA). The main requirement to become eligible for an HSA historically has been that the pre-retiree must be covered by a certain kind of high-deductible health plan that is specifically identified as an HSA-eligible account. The One Big Beautiful Bill expanded eligibility for HSAs so that individuals who are covered by a direct primary care service arrangement can qualify.[36] Also, if you are enrolled in a bronze

32. "How Are Annuity Withdrawals Taxed?" Kiplinger.com, Oct. 28, 2024, https://www. kiplinger.com/retirement/annuities/602248/how-annuities-are-taxed

33. "How is an Annuity Taxed?" Northwestern Mutual, Feb. 28, 2025, https://www.northwesternmutual.com/life-and-money/how-is-an-annuity-taxed/

34. "How Are Annuity Withdrawals Taxed?" Kiplinger.com, Oct. 28, 2024, https://www. kiplinger.com/retirement/annuities/602248/how-annuities-are-taxed

35. "How Are Annuity Withdrawals Taxed?" Kiplinger.com, Oct. 28, 2024, https://www. kiplinger.com/retirement/annuities/602248/how-annuities-are-taxed

36. "What the 'One Big Beautiful Bill' Means for FSAs and HSAs," Employee Benefits Corporation, July 7, 2025, https://www.ebcflex.com/one-big-beautiful-bill/

or catastrophic health plan offered through the Health Insurance Marketplace, you can also contribute to an HSA.[37] Finally, you can also contribute to an HSA if you receive telehealth and other remote care services before meeting the deductible. While contributing to the HSA, you will be able to claim a tax deduction, and contributions from your employer will not count towards your income. In 2025, HSA contribution limits are $4,400 for an individual and $8,750 for a family; those over age 50 can make a $1,000 catch-up contribution per year.[38]

But the true benefits of the HSA are grounded in the reality that they are not just singly tax deductible, but potentially triple tax deductible because they are then allowed to grow tax-free, and further when used on qualified medical expenses are withdrawn for these payments without having paid a cent in taxes on any of the money as long you follow the rules.[39] The IRS maintains a list of the expenses that are eligible for HSA reimbursement, which includes long-term health insurance premiums, flu shots, physical therapy, therapy, hearing aids, glasses, many over the counter medications, and much more.[40]

One of the major benefits of establishing and funding an HSA is to save money for health expenses in retirement. In other words, instead of establishing an HSA and using all of the money to pay current healthcare expenses, you save at least a portion of this money for your healthcare expenses in retirement. While you cannot continue to contribute to an HSA once you sign up for Medicare at age 65, you can continue to use the dollars you previously contributed to an HSA to fund eligible expenses in retirement. You can also invest those funds so that they can potentially grow until you need them to pay

---

37. "What the 'One Big Beautiful Bill' Means for FSAs and HSAs," Employee Benefits Corporation, July 7, 2025, https://www.ebcflex.com/one-big-beautiful-bill/

38. "HSA Contribution Limits and Eligibility Rules for 2025 and 2026," Fidelity, https://www.fidelity.com/learning-center/smart-money/hsa-contribution-limits.

39. "HSA Triple Tax Advantages Explained," Fidelity, March 3, 2025, https://www.fidelity.com/learning-center/smart-money/are-hsa-contributions-tax-deductible

40. "HSA Qualified Expenses, Priority Health, Feb. 25, 2025, https://www.priority health.com/member/paying-for-care/health-savings-accounts/qualified-expenses

for health expenses in retirement. Note that withdrawals for non-qualified expenses will be taxed and may even incur an additional 10% IRS penalty.

DIVERSIFY YOUR RETIREMENT BY TAXABILITY

The point of looking into all of these strategies is the same point that has been discussed throughout the chapter: to enjoy retirement without the risk of running out of money. There are three main categories that should be addressed robustly to set yourself up in this way, and these are tax-deferred, tax-free, and taxable, which refer to taxes that will be paid on the accumulated wealth from the investment.

The tax-deferred category is primarily composed of the more conventional traditional IRA and 401(k) plans where the taxes are paid upon withdrawal of funds. The second category is the tax-free accounts, which include the Roth IRA and HSAs, as well as the life insurance class where the benefit will be paid out tax free to the beneficiary.

The last category, taxable, refers to everything that doesn't fit into the other categories—money you have paid income tax on goes in, and capital gains are taxed yearly. The reason for attending to the first two categories while also not avoiding the third, in one word is diversification. That diversification allows for flexibility which can help you better adapt to situations, expected or not, that present themselves in retirement.

This flexibility can offer greater control. You cannot control the markets, tax code, how long your retirement is, but you can provide yourself with greater flexibility that helps give you options on how to respond to anything that happens.

Taxes don't go away, and as I've established, for many people they may even become an even greater burden in retirement, so it is crucial to create as many avenues for tax mitigation as possible through this diversification process. This not only helps retirees to carry more money and flexibility into retirement, but also to potentially stretch that money over a longer period of time and maintain more control and flexibility when it comes to estate planning.

NEXT UP

Now that you have learned about the importance of having a tax strategy for retirement, in the next chapter we will talk about creating retirement income streams.

8

CREATING A RETIREMENT INCOME STREAM

In my practice, I've found that retirement satisfaction is strongly correlated with guaranteed income. In other words, what I've observed is that retirees with a higher percentage of guaranteed income than non-guaranteed income seem to spend more than those with the equivalent amount of non-annuitized wealth. This suggests that the form in which you hold your wealth may be more important in some cases than the raw number. In other words, a strategy of drawing down savings from a retirement nest egg invested in assets such as stocks and bonds may not encourage retirees to spend so that they can fully enjoy their retirement journey.

Today, the challenge in retirement planning is that retirees must plan for a longer retirement than previous generations, with fewer sources of lifelong income available. Pensions are not common in many workplaces these days. In fact, the U.S Bureau of Labor Statistics reports that only 15% of private industry workers had access to a defined benefit retirement plan, or pension, in 2023, the most recent year statistics are available.[1] In contrast, 60% of public sector workers

1. "15 percent of private industry workers had access to a defined pension retirement benefit plan," U.S. Bureau of Labor Statistics, April 19, 2024, https://www.bls.gov/opub/ted/2024/15-percent-of-private-industry-workers-had-access-to-a-defined-benefit-retirement-plan.htm

have access to a pension.[2] The shifting climate of retirement plan funding away from pensions and towards defined-benefit plans such as 401(k)s and 403(b)s, which has been happening for decades, means that most individuals and couples preparing for retirement must look towards other sources to supply the appropriate amount of guaranteed income in retirement.[3]

This involves using part of your retirement savings to generate income. In combination with Social Security and other sources, this makes it less likely that you will exhaust your savings. As it happens, nearly two in three Americans worry about running out of money while they're alive more than they worry about death, particularly among the Baby Boomer and Generation X cohort in or approaching retirement.[4]

Let's look at the case of a fictitious couple called Bernie and Grace, who did not have a retirement income stream other than Social Security. That wasn't uncommon when they retired in the late 1980s when very few people planned the way we plan now. But they were constantly worried about outliving their money, becoming a burden on their family or having to live in a nursing home on Medicaid. Bernie did experience significant health problems as he aged. Due to mobility problems and a recurring infection, he needed at-home healthcare aides to assist him for 16 hours a day for the last 18 months of his life. Although he had a small long-term care insurance policy, that policy only paid a benefit of $75 a day, which was less than 25% of what a paid

---

2. "America's Public Sector Employees are Happy at Work, but the Majority Aren't Confident They are on Track for the Retirement They Envision," Corebridge Financial, July 25, 2024, https://investors.corebridgefinancial.com/news/news-details/2024/Americas-Public-Sector-Employees-Are-Happy-at-Work-But-Majority-Arent-Confident-They-Are-on-Track-for-the-Retirement-They-Envision/default.aspx

3. "One Key Element Leads to Increased Happiness in Retirement—3 Ways to Get It," CNBC, Nov. 29, 2024: https://www.cnbc.com/2024/11/29/key-elements-for-retirement-wellbeing.html

4. "Americans Are More Worried About Running Out of Money than Death," Allianz Life Insurance Company of North America, Apr. 22, 2025: https://www.allianzlife.com/about/newsroom/2025-Press-Releases/Americans-Are-More-Worried-About-Running-Out-of-Money-Than-Death

home healthcare aide cost. The long-term care policy did not cover his children helping with his care.

As it happened, even with their health challenges and a haphazard drawdown strategy, they died at ages 93 and 90 respectively and were able to leave a not insubstantial legacy. But they were lucky, unlike many in their generation who never systematically planned for retirement income. Wouldn't Bernie and Grace have been happier through their long retirement if they hadn't felt the need to worry about running out of money?

This chapter is all about creating a retirement income stream that will allow you to cover your expenses and discretionary needs without rapidly drawing down your savings. First, we'll look, briefly, at some of the main sources of income in retirement, then at constructing a retirement income stream. These have both been covered at length in previous chapters, so the main emphasis here is on the factors and risks to consider in constructing income for today and the rest of your retirement. In the conclusion, I'll sum up the strategy I've outlined in this and previous chapters and talk about what has drawn me to my profession.

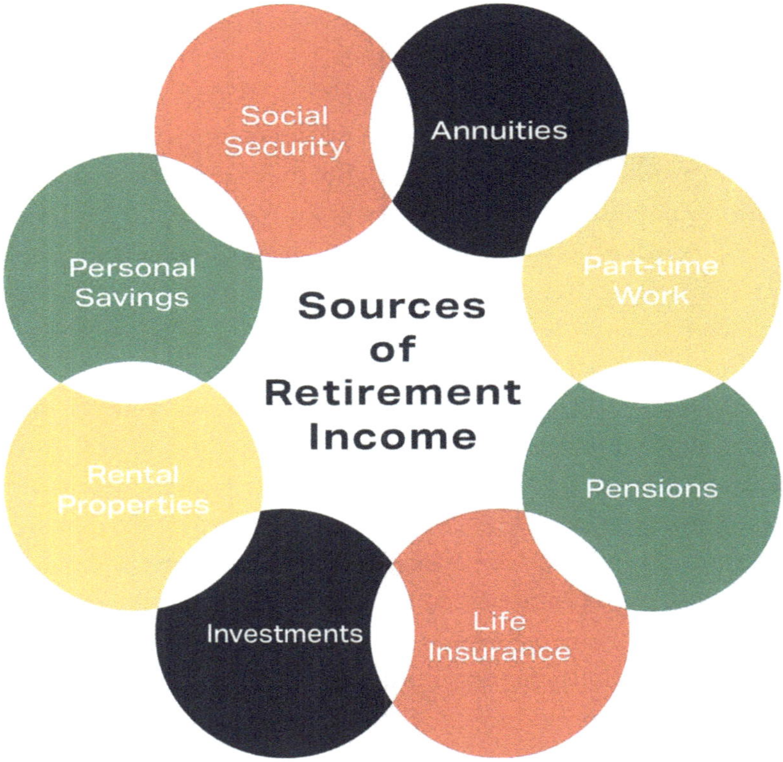

There are several potential sources of retirement income, so let's take a closer look at a few of them. Of course, the sources that make sense for each individual will vary by their unique financial circumstances.

Social Security. This covers, on average, about 40% of the typical amount a retiree needs to pay their bills.[5] In Chapter 6, I discussed some of the key filing factors like age, health, income and whether you're married, single, divorced or widowed. All these need to be considered to help you maximize your monthly benefit and align it with your overall retirement income strategy.

---

5. "The Data is Very Clear: One Key Element Leads to Increased Happiness in Retirement—3 Ways to Get It," CNBC.com, Fri., Nov. 29, 2024, https://www.cnbc.com/2024/11/ 29/key-elements-for-retirement-wellbeing.html

Fixed Income Annuities (FIAs). I covered these in Chapter 5. You give a lump-sum of money or a series of premium payments to an insurance company in exchange for a guaranteed retirement income payment. Annuities, including FIAs, offer steady money which can be relied on and have some—though not complete—potential for interest credits tied to an external index with protection from downside losses.[6] Like Social Security, depending on your age, health and the type of contract you have, it can be advantageous to turn this on later when you have the option, since there is potential for growth over time. All guarantees are backed by the financial strength of the issuing company.

Permanent Life Insurance. A cash value, or "permanent," life insurance policy provides not only a death benefit but may also provide retirement income because the premiums you pay help create a cash value component within the policy. These funds may be accessed for additional income in retirement if needed.

Pensions. As I've just said, few people have these anymore. The veterans, teachers, police officers, firefighters and so on who still get a guaranteed pension certainly treasure this part of their reliable retirement income. If you are one of the vanishing breeds with a private-sector pension, the most important thing is understanding your options and how to manage these funds for retirement income. The money isn't yours until you retire. In some situations, it could be taken away or modified if the company that sponsors the pension goes bankrupt, changes ownership or switches to a defined contribution plan such as a 401(k) or 403(b). Be sure to understand and discuss all of your option before making such an important retirement decision.

Rental Property Income. This isn't all that common either, but some of my clients have invested in rental property as a retirement income tool. The rental income they receive, minus the costs of

---

6. "Fixed Index and Buffer Annuities Explained," Fidelity, Sept. 23, 2024, https://www.fidelity.com/learning-center/personal-finance/retirement/fixed-indexed-annuity

property improvements, repairs and taxes, can contribute a regular stream of income to their retirement income plan.

Wealth Management Sources. There are two types: dividends from stocks, stock mutual funds or stock exchange-traded funds (ETFs), and interest from certificates of deposit, bonds, bond mutual funds or bond ETFs. With planning, dividends, especially those from companies with a record of increasing dividends over time, can form part of a retirement paycheck. Bonds, bond funds and bond ETFs, along with certificates of deposit, can also provide part of a retirement paycheck.

As we've seen, it's usually preferable to create retirement income from a variety of income sources to help you maximize growth as well as your payout. Another fictitious couple, Victor and Marianne, served in the military for decades. They decided to stay in the military at least 20 years to get the pension. What they did not expect is that during those 20 years, they kept getting promoted, and they both retired as colonels, which meant they were in line to receive a pension much bigger than they had anticipated. Marianne was also a breast cancer survivor, which meant that she retired with 100% disability. That status gave her an additional $4,000 a month in disability benefits that was not subject to taxes.

Because of their desire to maximize their current income, they decided not to enroll in the Survivor Benefit Plan to provide for each other when they died.[7] By waiting to claim Social Security later and deferring taking any money from their combined $1 million that they contributed to Thrift Savings Plan accounts, they have guaranteed income sources in the form of Social Security plus invested money that they rolled over into IRAs from the Thrift Savings Plan.

---

7. "Military survivor benefits and life insurance," USA.gov, March 18, 2025, https://www.usa.gov/military-survivor-benefits

CONSTRUCTING A RETIREMENT INCOME STREAM

From the specific combination of assets you can draw on (for example: Social Security, one pension, one IRA and a couple rental properties; or Social Security, two IRAs, a fixed income annuity and some dividends) you construct your retirement income stream. I've already covered this as well, but to reiterate: The process is to match your monthly discretionary and non-discretionary expenses in terms of income with your different income streams.

One thing I should highlight is the 4% Rule, which a group of retirement financial advisors relied on—and some still do. Based on historical market data, research and actuarial tables, they had found that it was possible to spend 4% of your savings annually in retirement, and that growth in investments could make up the rest and you wouldn't have to worry about running out of money before you died. There are ways to calculate your chances of running out of money used this methodology based on Monte Carlo simulations. These simulations are computer based models that show a variety of scenarios to predict the likelihood of a successful retirement—in this case, the probability that a 4% withdrawal rate will last for an entire retirement of a specific duration.[8] I don't like this methodology. Why? All too often, there is a decent probability that a 4% drawdown in assets over a retirement results in running of money, especially since that rule is based on market data from decades ago which is likely not relevant today. The probability might not be that high, but all the same, I'd prefer none of my clients have to face it. I also want to avoid significant asset drawdown whenever possible.

8. "What is a Monte Carlo Simulation?" Modern Wealth Management, Feb. 3, 2025, https://www.modwm.com/what-is-a-monte-carlo-simulation/

FACTORS TO CONSIDER IN CONSTRUCTING INCOME FOR TODAY AND THE REST OF YOUR RETIREMENT

Inflation Risk: Because of inflation, retirees end up spending more over time for the same goods and services while their income doesn't usually rise in a commensurate way. In most cases, Social Security is the exception, as it has the potential to be adjusted for inflation. While the high inflation of 2021 and 2022 subsided by 2024 and 2025, that only meant that inflation was not rising as quickly going forward. Prices didn't fall back to pre-pandemic levels.[9]

Going forward, inflation, like other risks in retirement, is unknown. Inflation could stay moderate as it did for decades, or it might spike due to a number of factors, such as trade tariffs, government debt, rising wages or corporate price increases. A sustainable retirement income plan will take inflation into consideration and attempt to mitigate it, potentially through investment of part of the portfolio into growth investments designed to help beat inflation and other investments that may at least keep up with the rate of inflation.

Longevity Risk: Longevity risk is a problem that this whole book addresses: the risk of outliving your money. While it is a real concern, there are also examples like Bernie and Grace, who didn't run out of money, but the worry that they would run out significantly compromised how much they enjoyed their retirement.

I believe that the key to dealing with longevity risk is a robust, multi-faceted retirement income plan. There is no one single solution to longevity risk—outside of a large amount of wealth—so for everyone else, retirement planning based on your unique retirement journey, goals, current financial situation and retirement savings is the way to go. Most of the risks of retirement boil down to issues that are outside of our control—health, inflation, need for long-term care and more—so the best we can do is to make the calculated moves designed to

---

9. "Why Inflation Is Still a Problem for Today's Retirees," Morningstar, Jul. 9, 2024: https://www.morningstar.com/retirement/why-inflation-is-still-problem-todays-retirees

provide the money you need for each of these things by planning with a good margin for error.

Death of a Spouse Risk: Many couples I encounter in my practice, either pre-retirement or in retirement, consist of a main bread-winner and a homemaker. A hypothetical couple I'll call Jim and Eileen, which demonstrates this type of client, built their retirement income plan around Jim's pension, which they took without a survivor's benefit. That meant when Jim passed away due to a sudden heart attack, most of their income was gone. Eileen did still have Jim's Social Security benefit and a modest pot of retirement savings, which consisted of $250,000 invested in the stock market. I might help someone like Eileen reposition her investment assets to provide some income and also talk her through the implications of downsizing her home.

Eileen, like many other widows, would pay the triple "widow's penalty" upon Jim's death. First, she went from two Social Security checks to receiving just one, so even though she kept Jim's, it was a significant loss of income. Second, she lost his pension income, as I've discussed. Third, after the grace period for filing taxes jointly passed, she got dropped into a higher tax bracket as a single person.[10]

The plans that Jim and Eileen made were premised on the income of the breadwinner, because the homemaker didn't have much to contribute financially. If one day he has a fatal heart attack, what happens to her? The only way to help overcome this, financially as well as emotionally, is to plan for it happening well ahead of time. There are ways to avoid the harshest versions of the widow's penalty.

For example, Roth conversions might help drop the survivor's income low enough to mitigate the tax aspect. Proper Social Security planning, as discussed in Chapter 6, can also make a big difference. If Jim had waited to claim until age 70, instead of at age 65, Eileen would have had a larger benefit by 40%, but because they didn't think that

---

10. "Widow's Penalty: Three Ways to Protect Your Finances," Kiplinger, Apr. 10, 2025: https://www.kiplinger.com/retirement/widows-penalty-how-to-protect-your-finances

Jim would pass at such a relatively young age of 74, they didn't consider this option.

Healthcare Risk: The risk of cancer increases with age. In fact, the National Cancer Institute's statistics reveal that while only 26 people out of 100,000 under age 20 will be diagnosed with cancer, nearly 2,000 out of 100,000 will be diagnosed with cancer from ages 70 to 74.[11] Consider how a cancer diagnosis not only upends a retiree's life, but also potentially their finances. Another fictional couple, Julia and Darryl, faced this scenario. An initial Stage 1 cancer diagnosis was later found to be Stage 3, which forced them to adjust their retirement plans.

Needless to say, what Julia and Darryl had to deal with in a short sequence is something faced by millions of people every year, whether that's with cancer or another life-threatening, long-term illness like ALS, for example. These scenarios, the bad ones and the worst ones, happen to people every day. You go into the doctor for a routine check-up, there's some tests—suddenly your whole life changes, and your retirement plan must change along with it.

As they found out, having cancer is really expensive, even with good insurance. The cost of some cancer therapies can run into thousands of dollars a month in additional out-of-pocket costs for Medicare patients. Some elderly patients experience what Dr. Yousef Zafar of Duke University Hospital calls "financial toxicity:" fearing bankruptcy, some patients will forego their treatment entirely, not take their pills as often as they need to, or refrain from telling their specialist the full extent of their symptoms.[12]

The effects of cancer treatment can leave many people with cognitive deficits and in need of some caregiving.[13] For cancer patients,

---

11. "Age and Cancer Risk," U.S. National Cancer Institute, May 2, 2025, https://www.cancer.gov/about-cancer/causes-prevention/risk/age

12. "When Cancer Costs Too Much: Why Financial Toxicity Deserves a Place in Clinical Conversations," KevinMD.com, Sep. 17, 2025: https://kevinmd.com/2025/09/when-cancer-costs-too-much-why-financial-toxicity-deserves-a-place-in-clinical-conversations.html.

13. "Cancer-Related Cognitive Impairment: A Practical Guide for Oncologists," Journal of Clinical Oncology: Oncology Practice," March 5, 2025

the choices can be agonizing—do you forego treatment so that your spouse won't be left with a ton of medical debt or do you move forward hoping for a cure or at least a few more years? Health-care risk is the most obvious of the many risks that can throw off the best retirement plan, and again, we can only do so much planning for what often happens as a shock event.

Market Risk: Market risk appears at a lot of different stages of the process and can manifest in several different ways: a merger can happen in your employer, which causes them to lay you off earlier than you expected, and without the prospect of getting a well-paying job at this age, you might be forced to retire. Your portfolio might be heavily stock based, so what happens to those if a crash happens like in 2008 or 2020?[14] Without extensive planning, market downturns and crashes could mean trouble for you.

The main contributor to the 2020 stock market crash was the COVID-19 pandemic. After the global pandemic accelerated in the United States, lockdowns shut down businesses and curtailed travel in February 2020. The economy cratered into a recession, the stock market plunged.[15] During the crash, the S&P 500 fell by 30%, including a 12% decline on March 16, 2020.[16] Fortunately, and unlike during the Great Depression, swift intervention by Congress with a stimulus package and the Federal Reserve by cutting interest rates and quantitative easing deterred the worst possible outcome.[17] The pandemic brought home to everyone who lived through it how the unexpected disaster

---

14. "What We've Learned from 150 Years of Stock Market Crashes," Morningstar.com, June 12, 2025, https://www.morningstar.com/economy/what-weve-learned-150-years-stock-market-crashes

15. "What is a stock market crash?" SoFi.com, Nov. 18, 2024, https://www.sofi.com/learn/content/what-is-a-stock-market-crash/

16. "What is a stock market crash?" SoFi.com, Nov. 18, 2024, https://www.sofi.com/learn/content/what-is-a-stock-market-crash/

17. "Robust COVID Relief Bolstered Economy and Reduced Hardship for Millions," Center on Budget and Policy Priorities, March 6, 2023, https://www.cbpp.org/research/ poverty-and-inequality/robust-covid-relief-bolstered-economy-and-reduced-hardship-for

can happen at any time, and you know what they have to say about the best-laid plans.[18]

Long-Term Care Risk: Bernie, of Bernie and Grace, who I mentioned earlier, needed long-term and end-of-life care before his death. People who live to be his age (93) often have many health problems, and he was no exception. For a couple without a steady retirement income other than Social Security, that meant a lot of work and a lot of money. Thus, long-term care. It cost Bernie and Grace around $150,000 in those last 18 months of his life. Since again they didn't have a real retirement paycheck, their financial advisors were worried about spending so much, but it wasn't like Grace and his children and grandchildren would let him lie in bed all day, every day, until he died. In this situation, a fixed index annuity with a long-term care rider might be one option to help provide additional income to cover situations like the one that Bernie and Grace confronted.

Before you say anything, no, Medicare does *not* cover long-term care: This is a common misconception since Medicare does cover post-acute nursing home stays of up to 100 days—it won't help you if you need assistance with "non-medical" tasks.[19] Medicaid does provide some coverage, but of course you can only access that once you've significantly spent or drawn down your assets, which most of us would prefer to avoid if possible.[20]

Some statistics: More than half of seniors turning age 65 are expected to need some type of long-term care.[21] Those who need long-term care are anticipated to spend an average of $138,000 to obtain that

---

18. Laura Rodini, "What Was the COVID-19 Stock Market Crash of 2020? Causes and Effects," The Street, Nov. 10, 2022: https://www.thestreet.com/dictionary/covid-19-stock-market-crash-of-2020. Accessed Jun. 26, 2025.

19. The Kaiser Family Foundation found that nearly half of adults mistakenly believe this: Liz Hamel and Alex Montero, "The Affordability of Long-Term Care and Support Services: Findings from a KFF Survey," Kaiser Family Foundation, Nov. 14, 2023: https://www.kff.org/health-costs/poll-finding/the-affordability-of-long-term-care-and-support-services. Accessed Jun. 26, 2025.

20. "An Overview of Healthcare Risks in Retirement," Center for Retirement Research, Jan. 22, 2025, https://crr.bc.edu/an-overview-of-healthcare-risks-in-retirement/

21. "Long-term care statistics 2025," Feb. 6, 2024, https://www.consumeraffairs.com/health/long-term-care-statistics.html

care.[22] Seniors with chronic diseases, such as heart disease, are more likely to need long-term care.[23]

In my experience, long-term care is probably the biggest potential retirement need that people have the least money for. A lot of people will likely end up self-funding instead of getting an insurance policy. We advisors like to use the "bucket" approach. There would be, then, four buckets: the first bucket with 1-2 years living expenses; the second working on funding the next 5-8 years of cash flow; the third with a remainder of the portfolio that can be pulled from in emergencies; and a fourth bucket for long-term care expenses.

The cost of long-term care depends on the type of care (around-the-clock or part-time, for medical and/or non-medical needs, at-home versus in a facility) and how long you'd need it. Of course, it's very hard to predict any of these factors in advance, but you can do some things to frame an estimate: find facilities in the area you like and investigate the cost of care, check the rates of local agencies providing home health aides, for example. There are statistics, pretty grim ones, about how much long-term care we need. On average it's 2.2 years if you're a man and 3.7 if you're a woman (but relatively healthy people need care for longer).[24]

Asset allocation for the long-term care bucket often needs to be growth-oriented for most people due to the cost of long-term health care needs in a facility or at-home as those costs are likely to continue to increase. Your growth-oriented financial assets have the potential to increase to pay for long-term care if needed, as well as help you keep up with inflation. As for where to hold the assets, we might look at a traditional IRA as an example, because, first, they often already have

22. "Long-term care statistics 2025," Feb. 6, 2024, https://www.consumeraffairs.com/health/long-term-care-statistics.html

23. "Long-term care statistics 2025," SingleCare.com, Aug. 7, 2025, https://www.singlecare.com/blog/news/long-term-care-statistics/

24. "Worried About Long-Term-Care Expenses? Let's Do Something About It," Morningstar, Nov. 20, 2024: https://www.morningstar.com/retirement/youre-worried-about-long-term-care-expenses-lets-do-something-about-it.

one, and second, in some cases, healthcare expenses from a traditional IRA can be deducted from your income for tax purposes.[25]

Underspending Risk: Longevity risk has a lesser-known twin brother. I'll call him "underspending risk." You've heard the stories of the people who die without family, and it turns out they were secret millionaires? Like Geoffrey Holt, the caretaker of a mobile home park in New Hampshire, who left an estate worth $3.8 million to his hometown of Hinsdale. Or Doris Schwartz, a high-school French teacher in West York, Pennsylvania, who left $3.4 million to establish an education fund for underprivileged girls and women.[26]

Now that they've passed away, it's impossible to guess what they were thinking about in leaving such large sums without spending anything on themselves, even into retirement. It's one thing if your needs are genuinely simple, you don't have many close family members and you have a giving spirit.

Underspending risk might be, in some situations, the tendency of an obsessive miser, who won't spend anything on things that make them happy. *You shouldn't be depriving yourself, especially in retirement.* With a type of client like Victor and Marianne, the two retired colonels, I would tell them to treat themselves. I know they're frugal people, like most career military, but take that trip to Europe.

Think also of this type of client. Consider Will, a man who's approaching retirement age and who limits his shopping excessively, going only to Wal-Mart with the coupons he clipped, and frequently to Dollar General, which gives you a $5 off coupon weekly for spending at least $20. This isn't normal behavior, and I might urge a client with these tendencies to loosen up and change their ways. The point of having a well-established, detailed retirement financial strategy is that

---

25. "Worried About Long-Term-Care Expenses? Let's Do Something About It," Morningstar, Nov. 20, 2024: https://www.morningstar.com/retirement/youre-worried-about-long-term-care-expenses-lets-do-something-about-it.

26. "7 Secret Millionaires Who Left It All to Charity," Money Talks News, Apr. 17, 2025: https://www.moneytalksnews.com/slideshows/secret-millionaires-who-left-it-all-to-charity

you'll be able to trust it and spend the money you've saved for this very purpose, on the things you need and want.

NEXT UP

In this chapter, you've learned how we aim to mitigate risks through the intentional construction of an ongoing income stream from the different sources you have available. We do this by seeking to (a) optimize income through the sources, (b) manage expenses as they arise, (c) use investments and insurance products for the potential growth of savings outside of income, and (d) minimize taxes to maximize income.

As a retirement financial professional, my passion in writing this is to share what I know with as many retirees and people approaching retirement as possible. If you read this book and avoid even one of the many pitfalls I've pointed out, I'll have done my job. In my experience, there's not one of the problems I've described that can't be addressed through careful planning. When you feel as I do that God blessed you with the ability to help people, you have the duty to do it. Helping people to retire in a sustainable way is what the Lord has called me to do with my life.

In Chapter 9, Establishing a Legacy, you'll gain an understanding of how to pass on your legacy, including your assets and your values, to your family and favorite causes.

9

ESTABLISHING A LEGACY

What does "legacy" mean? In the crudest sense, it's the money, property, and possessions left to your heirs after you leave the earth. In the deeper senses, it's about how you are remembered by your family, friends, acquaintances and even complete strangers who your financial legacy may impact. In other words, your larger impact on the world.

I'm going to start this chapter with some personal reflections on how I view my own legacy, because these beliefs and values deeply inform how I help my clients to mold their own legacies. In the second part, I discuss how you create your legacy in conjunction with the overall strategy to retire. In the third and fourth, I return to the nuts and bolts of how to go about doing this financially and legally.

MY LEGACY

My personal legacy includes my husband, children, grandchildren and extended family. It has been exemplified by creating a lasting legacy for my family—one that nurtures personal growth, a financially stable legacy and a spirit of servant leadership. I intentionally started my firm with the goal of helping my family and community.

It's meta: My own personal and professional legacy lies in helping others create and shape theirs. I believe that as I climb, I uplift others, which enhances my own legacy.

My professional legacy initially began, by meeting clients more than 20 years ago through my church. I found that I could practice these skills in a way that people could identify with and help themselves, their families and their communities. As my practice grew, I gained many clients who live throughout the nation. Because of the personal attention and service that I provided, in addition to the comprehensive financial and legacy planning, my practice continues to grow through referrals. I didn't start my practice as a business, but as an educational endeavor within my church, which is at the core of my community.

I started by educating my fellow parishioners, which became a valuable resource for my church community, the local community and pre-retirees throughout the nation regarding retirement and legacy planning. As time went on, other churches were interested in my services through them, other organizations, businesses, corporations and other financial professionals. My financial services help my clients to bridge the gap between pre-retirement and retirement, providing greater access to the benefits of financial planning.

In my church and many others, we have a tradition of servant leadership. "Whoever wants to become great among you must be your servant," as Jesus said, related in the Gospels of both Mark and Matthew. The pastor, for instance, is called by God to serve the community and guide their spiritual growth towards him. My team and I are servant leaders to many individuals nationwide—our services specifically focus on retirement and legacy finances.

I believe that others in the community and nationwide have entrusted this part of their finances to me and my team because of our vision, passion for the work, as well as our compassion for them. I educate and inform them to help ensure that people are not merely okay in retirement, but that they can create a plan that allows them to embark on a retirement journey knowing that they are capable of leaving financial, as well as moral legacies, to their families, churches and wider communities.

"To whom much is given, much is required" is a concept I live by. I also pass this same concept onto my clients. My team and I are very intentional very intentional about helping my clients build this legacy. I mean that at every stage of the process, when you're my client, I will do my best to ensure that you are well enough educated on these matters that you can explain them to your own family sitting around at the dinner table. In my experience of helping my clients articulate their own legacy, I've found it is tremendously empowering for them. They feel good about doing it.

I want to make sure my clients thoroughly understand their own legacy to the point of explaining what they're doing and why to anyone. That's why, for instance, I consistently ask my clients certain questions, so they can practice formulating their own legacy with me, to confirm that they know and understand thoroughly what the plans are, enough to explain it with confidence to their family and friends.

I've said it before, but it bears repeating: You only retire once. It's not a game that goes back to the start when you fail. Getting this wrong can be terrible. Consider, for example, the hypothetical case of a couple who decides to claim a pension without a survivor benefit to enjoy a larger income in retirement. If the spouse who holds the pension—usually the husband—dies sooner than expected, the wife could be left with significantly less income than she needs to main-tain the lifestyle that they have established. As a result of this misguided decision, a surviving spouse would have to significantly curtail his or her income.

There are many less dramatic mistakes that can still negatively impact your retirement. Consider another hypothetical case, this one of Tracy. She was worried that politicians would undermine Social Security, so she immediately claimed at age 62. However, she kept working, not realizing that for every $1 she made over the Social Security earnings limit, Social Security would take $2 of her benefit back, meaning that with her salary, she essentially didn't get a benefit at all.[1] By the time she realized her mistake, it was too late to change her Social Security claiming decision.[2] Tracy wasted an opportunity to obtain a larger benefit, which she could have received by waiting to claim. When she claimed at age 62, her benefit was $2,400 a month. If she had waited to claim until age 65, when she planned to retire, her benefit would have risen to $2,976 plus cost-of-living increases. Fortunately, her benefits are recalculated to reflect the withheld dollars once she reaches full retirement age.[3]

Potential situations like these demonstrate that you don't have a do-over on many retirement decisions and that you need help to decide how to make the most of your available resources. Retirement income planning is a discipline that isn't always easy or practical to pick up on the fly. To help you maximize your time and your finances, it can be very valuable to find me or someone like me who understands the process thoroughly, has plenty of practice in doing it, and is guided along the way by the values of the community you share.

This, in a very real sense, is my ongoing legacy, the way I strive to uplift my own community. It's revealed to me only in bits and pieces, through my meetings and chance encounters with clients. It happens when, for instance, someone in my church who I don't really know was referred to me by another member of the community 10 to 15 years ago, and they remembered my name and reputation when they started to think seriously about their retirement. It happens when one of my older clients walks a new one into the lobby and says, "Felicia will take great care of you."

---

1. "What happens if I work and get Social Security Retirement benefits?" U.S. Social Security Administration, Jan. 2, 2025, https://www.ssa.gov/faqs/en/questions/KA-01921.html

2. "Can I withdraw my Social Security retirement claim and reapply later to increase my benefit amount?" U.S. Social Security Administration, March 13, 2024, https://www.ssa.gov/faqs/en/questions/KA-01993.html

3. "Social Security Income Penalties are Refunded to You When You Reach Full Retirement Age," Greenbush Financial, Aug. 7, 2025, https://www.greenbushfinancial.com/all-blogs/social-security-income-penalty-refund

HOW TO CREATE A LEGACY

In conjunction with your retirement plan, we help you figure out what, how and when you want your legacy to be. Planning for retirement and legacy at the same time can be a delicate balance because they have different objectives. With retirement, we create plans designed to help provide you a lifetime income through managing risk, whereas with legacy, we are talking about a financial impact on your family and community. Legacy plans are meant to help create a foundation of wealth, which could help support family, future generations and your community.

GROWING YOUR LEGACY

There are situations in which the two types of planning contradict each other, and when that happens, I feel strongly that retirement has to come first. You can't compromise your lifetime income—you have to take care of yourself first. Think of the airplane announce-ments telling parents to put on their breathing apparatus before fixing that of their kid. Don't end up like my hypothetical client in Charlotte, who nearly spent all his savings on his daughter and her kids well in advance of retirement as you learned in Chapter 3.

Your legacy can be bigger than your family. Think about how you want to be remembered and by who. Lots of my clients I met through the church want to give the church part of their legacy. Many members of my church engage in missionary work; several have decided to leave money to the mission program so that it has the resources to continue for future generations. Others have different hobbies or causes they're involved in, including the environment, animal welfare, their alma mater, the library and adult literacy. These are the specific organizations you contributed to during your lifetime, which you really believe in, and which you want to contribute to after your time. With the resources that you have, and which will be available to you, what impact do you want to have on your family and your community?

Education is a big one for some people. They contribute part of their legacy to their university, or fraternity or sorority (as I plan to do). It doesn't even have to be your own educational experience. Bernie, for instance, had always really valued his Jesuit education, so when he died, he willed a small part of his legacy to the Red Cloud Indian School, operated by the Jesuits for Lakota kids on the Pine Ridge Indian Reservation, one of the poorest parts of the country, and asked for donations to the same in honor of his death.

Let's consider another hypothetical individual, Felix. Felix lived here in South Carolina his whole life. When he came to me to start thinking about his legacy, he had been captivated with his granddaughter's nursing career. She had a really good experience in the nursing program at Clemson, so what he decided that he wanted to do was to endow a scholarship for other nursing students like her—$5,000 per year that went to offset the tuition.

Other people have organizations they've contributed to and/or volunteered with. Another hypothetical lady, let's call her Cheryl, had learned to garden with a community gardening group that co-owned a piece of land for that purpose. When she died, she left $10,000 to that co-op and asked for donations in her memory, because she wanted that experience of growing and nurturing plants that would eventually end up on her family's table to be available to others.

THE ASSETS IN YOUR ESTATE

Figure out what assets you're going to leave behind. Besides your liquid assets, you have a house, maybe two? Family homes can be special, in some cases they've been in the family a long time, and it's important to some people that they stay this way.

This can be negative as well as positive. What *doesn't* your family want? For example, people used to use China for special occasions and each family had a set that might be passed down. That isn't really the case anymore, and a lot of people who assume their nice silverware will go to their kids encounter kids who don't want it. This applies especially to packrats and hoarders. Remember Cheryl? Her husband, Gregory, since he wasn't up to figuring out what was in each room of his house towards the end of his life, willed the belongings in them to specific grandchildren. As a result, one of his grandchildren ended up with all the spy and detective novels he'd read over the years. We're aiming for a more intentional approach than that.

Then there are the hoarders not by choice. Many couples downsize their homes in retirement. Let's think of the example of a couple who had started this process. They had a new place which they had started moving into when their health started going downhill, and as a result they never finished the move. So, when they passed, they left the empty condo and a house full of junk for their kids to figure out where all of it would go. In their case none of the kids wanted the family home or the condo, which made things that much more complicated. They were eventually able to coordinate with a professional who specialized in inventory and donation of the possessions they didn't want and who gave them receipts as a nice little tax write-off, but it would have been better to have the conversation with their parents and an exact determination beforehand.

One thing that will be especially important for future legacy-givers is digital assets: electronic files, email, social media accounts, all that stuff. People who are now in their 40s and 50s—and even 60s and 70s—definitely have digital assets and will want to incorporate them into their legacy planning. You at least don't want your kids failing to figure out all your passwords. With your OS (Apple, Microsoft or Linux) you can take steps here and now to control what happens to these. For example, Apple allows you to designate individuals who can receive your log-in information to your iCloud storage and the apps connected to that storage such as your email, contacts and texts.[4] You can arrange for your heirs to get access, and your advisor can help with this by being involved and aware of what's happening, where to send the death certificate to and any other arrangements you need to make.

Probably at least some Facebook friends, even if you're not that close, would appreciate knowing that you're not around anymore. You can set it up with a loved one to transform your page into an online memorial. But you have to figure that out in advance, or Facebook won't let you do it. Otherwise, long after you're dead those birthday greetings from people you don't really know will keep pouring in.[5]

Have conversations with your family members about who is going to get what, from the house or houses down to the little knick-knacks if necessary. Be as transparent as possible. If you don't have these

---

4. "How to Add a Legacy Contact for Your Apple Account," Apple.com, Nov. 13, 2024, https://support.apple.com/en-us/102631

5. "What Digital Assets Should I Include in an Estate Plan?" SuperLawyers, Jun. 27, 2025: https://www.superlawyers.com/resources/estate-planning-and-probate/what-digital-assets-should-i-include-in-an-estate-plan.

conversations in advance, you leave things to chance, which can lead to acrimony, and that's not a legacy you want.

It's the fortunate family that doesn't fight over possessions after a loved one dies, and a lot of families aren't fortunate. Then there is the fictional example of another couple, Cheryl, who pre-deceased Gregory by almost a decade. One of their daughters had preemptively decided that her own daughter should inherit her mother's jewelry and took it without consulting anyone when Cheryl died. She had similar designs on some of Gregory's property. And it ended with her brother, who as executor, was obliged to follow the letter of Gregory's will, being forced to change the locks on the home they grew up in to stop his sister from taking things.

In some cases, clients with substantial assets may be able to see the impact of their legacy before they go. A good way for some families with a lot, who want to pay it forward, can use what is called a Donor-Advised Fund (DAF). Under this type of legacy account, which is tax-advantaged incidentally, they can get together with a 501c3 charity to establish a fund which they set the priorities for giving and which the charity will manage on their behalf.[6] Whatever the beneficiary may be—a university, a church, another kind of organization—you can see in real time your contribution helping others.

ESTATE PLANNING

I want to start this section by saying that I am not an attorney, and I don't give estate planning advice or legal services. But no holistic retirement plan is complete without estate planning, so it's here where we work closely with estate planning attorneys to integrate this important component into our clients' retirement plans.

---

6. "Philanthropy and Wealth Planning: How to Build a Charitable Giving Strategy," First Western Trust, Dec. 15, 2024: https://myfw.com/articles/philanthropy-and-wealth-planning-how-to-build-a-charitable-giving-strategy. Accessed Jun. 9, 2025; "Top Tools for HNW Philanthropy," Foundation Source: https://foundationsource.com/resources/articles/top-tools-for-hnw-philanthropy. Accessed Jun. 9, 2025.

Let's talk about what no one wants to talk about, which is absolutely necessary and that most people avoid thinking about: documents. The will comes first, obviously. You need to make sure that you not only have an up-to-date will, but that it's readily available to your heirs when your time comes. Of course, the lawyer who writes it will have the original, but what if your estate attorney retires or passes away themselves? What happens if the firm goes out of business, merges with another practice, or sets up in a different state?

Transfer on Death (TOD) designations are a legal tool that many people aren't aware of but should be. Liquid assets, checking and savings accounts can be immediately transferred to your beneficiaries through signing specific beneficiary forms with your bank, brokerage firm or financial advisor.[7] This can happen as soon as the death certificate is presented, and it's a good idea to have your estate planner involved with the process. The main benefit is that it avoids probate, which we will discuss soon. A similar document for property, like the family home can be drawn up. In South Carolina they're called life estate deeds, but names vary with the state.

Who are your beneficiaries? Your spouse, kids, siblings, further removed family, and/or the church, organizations, causes you want your legacy to benefit? You probably know, but it's important to get it certified and updated should this change because otherwise someone may inherit your property that you didn't intend to. You may have heard about Jeffrey Rollson. In 1987, when he was expecting to get married to his then-girlfriend, he designated her as beneficiary of his IRA on his employer's form. They broke up a few years later, but he never updated this information even in his will. When he died, this random ex had a legal claim to his IRA, now worth in excess of $1 million, and though his brothers contested the claim federally, law is about what was written, and Jeffrey never wrote his wishes down, so the courts

7. "Transfer on Death (TOD): What It Is and How It Helps Loved Ones Avoid Probate," Investopedia, March 10, 2025, https://www.investopedia.com/terms/t/trans ferondeath.asp

sided with the ex.[8] This shows how important it is to keep your will and other documents updated as marriage, divorce, re-marriage and death happen.

Another type of document is the trust. A trust is a powerful legal tool that enables you to provide your spouse, children or other heirs with your legacy after you are gone. If you are worried about passing before your kids are old enough to manage money, or if you want to provide for a sibling who's never been good with money, for instance, trusts are helpful, because they can be managed by a trusted attorney, CPA or estate planner rather than the direct beneficiary.

You can write them into your will (what's called a testamentary trust) or establish them directly when you're alive (a living trust). The other main distinction is between revocable trusts that is to say, those that can be amended or shut down while you still have the power, and irrevocable trusts, which are a figurative "black box" from the time of signature until after your death.[9] Like a lot of the other documents, trust law varies in every state, and it's important to have a legal professional on board who thoroughly understands the law.

All the documents we're talking about help to minimize probate. Probate is the legal process of transferring your property to your heirs. The better you specify your wishes through legally certified documents, the less probate your heirs will have to go through, which is good news, because probate can be long and expensive.

Probate is also a public legal process that is monitored by real estate agents and all other sorts of vultures. There is no privacy when it comes to probate, and they will be calling your heirs, sending them postcards and letters inquiring about property you left them especially. Best to make it as pain-free—that is to say, short—as possible.

---

8. "They Broke Up in 1989, But Now His Ex-Girlfriend Is Inheriting His $1 Million Retirement Account After 40 Years," Yahoo! Finance, Jun. 14, 2024: https://finance.yahoo.com/news/broke-1989-now-ex-girlfriend-133011668.html.

9. "Understanding the Different Types of Trusts," Western & Southern Financial Group, May 21, 2025: https://www.westernsouthern.com/retirement/what-are-the-different-types-of-trusts. Accessed Jul. 26, 2025.

Taxes on estates deserve a mention. As of this writing, the One Big Beautiful Bill Act signed by President Trump has increased the exemption from federal estate taxes to $15 million in assets, which will now be indexed to inflation.[10] This is good news for very high net worth families, although it doesn't go all the way and abolish the federal estate tax altogether, as some were hoping for. Also, some states—not South Carolina, fortunately—continue to tax estates at varying rates and levels of exemption.[11]

If you are leaving behind assets in an IRA, we still have to reckon with the effects of President Biden's SECURE Act 2.0, which eliminated the "stretch IRA" exemption for most beneficiaries except spouses. This means that if you leave an IRA to your kids or other heirs, they are required to take its distributions over no longer than 10 years after your death. Remember that they will owe taxes on these distributions and consider whether you can help ease this pain by a preemptive Roth conversion.

Some final documents to consider are the financial power of attorney and a healthcare power of attorney. If you are married, most people generally choose their spouse to be responsible as both your financial and healthcare power of attorney, so that they can make both financial and healthcare decisions on your behalf. If you are single, divorced or widowed, the decisions become more complicated. If you have adult children, they may be worth considering too. Consider another hypothetical case. Anna was divorced with two grown sons. Her younger son Peter was in medical school, so it made sense for her to choose Peter as her healthcare power of attorney. Her older son Will was a college professor, and she chose him for her financial power of attorney. She discussed the responsibilities with each son and made

---

10. ""IRS Releases Tax Inflation Adjustment for Tax Year 2026, Including Amendments from the One Big Beautiful Bill," U.S. internal Revenue Service, Oct. 9, 2025, https:// www.irs.gov/newsroom/irs-releases-tax-inflation-adjustments-for-tax-year-2026-including-amendments-from-the-one-big-beautiful-bill

11. "New Law Increases Big Beyond-The-Grave Tax Break for the Wealthy," CNN, Jul. 20, 2025: https://www.cnn.com/2025/07/20/business/new-tax-law-increases-federal-estate-tax-exemption. Accessed

sure to keep them fully informed about all of her decision making so they felt included and understood her reasoning and her wishes.

The specifics of financial and health care power of attorney are dependent upon the laws in each state. In South Carolina, you can create a healthcare and/or financial power of attorney that allows a designated individual to handle your financial or business matters. Your document must be signed by two witnesses and notarized for it to be effective.[12] In South Carolina, your financial or healthcare power of attorney must be filed with the lands records office in the county where you live.[13]

There is much more I could say about the financial power of attorney, but from what I've written up to now it should be clear to you already that this is also a hefty responsibility to be placed with a trustworthy person. Because once you become incapacitated (this is what the "durable" refers to) that person has total control over what happens to your assets.[14]

A healthcare power of attorney is important to consider and establish from a legacy point of view because part of your legacy is the memories your loved ones have of your last days. You designate a friend, family member or members who control what happens to you after you're incapacitated.[15] It's best to get your wishes out in the open because that way you can limit what happens in your absence. Many people don't want to be kept alive on a ventilator, but if the person with your healthcare POA wants the doctors to do this and you're unable to correct them, then the doctors have to follow their wishes. Also, they can control what happens to your mortal remains. If you have a religious objection to organ donation, for instance, it's important to

---

12. "Power of Attorney Lawyers," Law Office of Rhett Burney, July 1, 2025, https://rhettburney.com/estate-planning/power-of-attorney/

13. "Power of Attorney Lawyers," Law Office of Rhett Burney, July 1, 2025, https://rhettburney.com/estate-planning/power-of-attorney/

14. "Financial Power of Attorney: Definition, Required Forms, and Example," Investopedia.com, March 12, 2025, https://www.investopedia.com/terms/f/financial-power-attorney.asp

15. "What is a Health Care Power of Attorney?" Investopedia.com, Sept. 5, 2024. https:// www.investopedia.com/terms/h/hcpa.asp

have your healthcare POA with someone who will respect this wish. If you don't have a spouse or children, you'll have to consider carefully who might be willing to fulfill this responsibility.

Consider the hypothetical case of Jill. Jill is a 48-year-old scientist who was diagnosed with Huntington's Disease, a fatal and progressive congenital illness.[16] Jill, who was single and had no children, had great friends in her lab, and two of them agreed to act as her health-care power of attorney while a third agreed to be her financial power of attorney. Jill had a group of physicians who were experts in her disease and who kept her and her friends informed about the progression and the impact of the disease on her functioning and mental faculties. Huntington's disease, which has a life expectancy of 10 to 30 years, causes involuntary movements, cognitive decline and depression, symptoms that worsen over time.[17]

Wills, trusts and healthcare and financial powers of attorney need to be drawn up in consultation with an attorney who knows estate law, and it's always a good idea to have your financial advisor in the loop on the financial side.

Also, keep documents safe. Most people—I hope—have a valid copy of their will in a file cabinet. A safety deposit box is often better, because it's more durable and your heirs are more likely to know where to find it. A will that no one can find is worth the same as one that doesn't exist. In some places (not here, in South Carolina unfortunately) you can deposit your will with the county where you live so when you pass, your will is already in possession of the relevant authorities.

I'm a firm believer that wills, transfer-on-death provisions, trusts, retirement plan and insurance policy beneficiary designations, and durable power of attorney documents should be reviewed every 10 years at minimum. Sometimes things will happen, like a death, marriage,

---

16. "Huntington's Disease," The U.S. National Institute of Neurological Disorders and Stroke, April 8, 2025, https://www.ninds.nih.gov/health-information/disorders/huntingtons-disease

17. "Huntington's Disease," Mayo Clinic, April 25, 2024, https://www.mayoclinic.org/diseases-conditions/huntingtons-disease/symptoms-causes/syc-20356117

divorce or remarriage that will definitely impact your legacy planning. You do not want your heirs to end up in the position of Jeffrey Rollson's brothers, who didn't inherit their brother's estate due to an outdated retirement plan beneficiary designation.

A less extreme case might be remarriage. Remarriage can be tough because it often involves hurt feelings (your own, your ex-spouse, your current spouse, and especially your children). If you don't make your wishes clear through these documents, a scenario could come up in which your kids, who never reconciled themselves to your remarrying, kick your spouse out of the house you shared. I've encountered this in my practice, and unfortunately, if a will wasn't updated to include a current spouse when the owner passed, and kids don't waive their interest, probate is required to follow the bloodline heirs. Make sure that doesn't happen by having your wishes ratified legally. Or you might have stepchildren now. Do you want them to inherit? All this requires thinking and rethinking as relationships change.

UP NEXT

I named my firm "Legacy Financial Advisors" because I recognize legacies—financial, material, and immaterial—as an intrinsic part of the holistic planning process for retirement. Legacy is the end of the journey you start in retirement. It's the destination, and you have to plan a journey appropriate to where you want to end up.

10

FINDING JOY IN THE JOURNEY: FINANCIAL FREEDOM

What does it mean to live a good life? We all want to be productive, have a rewarding job, be part of a community, and have the opportunity to raise a family, own a home and retire. But what is it really all for? What makes all of the sacrifice worth it? Although I am obviously biased, what makes it worthwhile for me is knowing that if I help you make the right choices, there will be a time in your life when you'll have your burdens relieved, gain peace of mind in an uncertain world, and attain the freedom that you've longed for in the form of a worry-free retirement. In a word, it's having freedom. Now as we know, freedom isn't free, so our working life is the price we pay, a downpayment on the freedom we earn when we retire. So, congratulations for being at the point where you are taking your courageous final steps towards that reward.

My job is not just to get the numbers right. Sure, it's an essential part—but what I enjoy equally, and what I feel sets me apart, is my focus on empowering my clients to maximize that reward. We work hard to help maximize the value of each dollar stored away, but those dollars become meaningful when we put them to work in a way where you have the say over how every second of your day is used. I get to figure out how to help you make each of those moments happy ones. Without that happiness, without that joy, the numbers don't have as much meaning as they otherwise could.

And it's not just that I enjoy doing it, it's that clients, such as yourself, will have a better retirement when I'm focused on your joy. People are only able to enjoy when they can get their minds off of the minutiae and onto the enjoyable thing. You'll find that it is easier to let go when you're supported by an empathetic, supportive advisor—someone who is emotionally invested in your journey and shares your goals.

You also want an advisor who watches the bottom line. It's all well and good to make hay while the sun is shining, put your money to work, but in retirement risk is king. That's another step towards that peace of mind that can be so elusive. To strike the right balance between risk mitigation and legacy for loved ones is a very delicate balancing act, and you only have one chance. This is a journey to be treasured, and that can only be accomplished if you spend your time doing the things you love and have the peace of mind to know your plans for your assets are being executed in the most thoughtful and impactful manner possible.

I believe that attaining financial freedom has four discrete but interrelated steps. The first step in attaining financial freedom is having sufficient sources of guaranteed income. There are many ways to do this, but the right way for you and your specific mix of assets will be different from everyone else's. The second step is to mitigate risk, that is, to create guardrails that make it difficult for the circumstances of the world to negatively impact the financial freedom you have attained. Financial risk isn't the only type of risk you face, as you also must navigate the complexities of balancing what to do with your freedom with how long that freedom will last, which is dependent upon your health. The sooner we start planning, the more options we can explore. And those options are crucial in the third step, which is legacy and estate planning. This is an important component to having peace of mind that some people do not anticipate, because it is more complicated than putting cash away in investment portfolios. To make sure your loved ones and the causes you are passionate about will be well taken care of after you are gone is not at the top of most retirees' lists, but I can't tell you how many times it ends up being so crucial to unlocking that freedom mindset. Overall, these steps help bring you to the finish, or to step four, which ultimately is just the beginning—experiencing the feeling of real freedom for the first time.

TRUE RETIREMENT FREEDOM

Most financial advisors have access to many of the same resources in this age of advanced financial technology. What we believe sets our services apart is that you are our priority. That goes for all of the details, not just the personal touch while assembling a portfolio of assets but that person-to-person availability and personality that is so often missing in the spreadsheet-based world of finance. Everything I do, I do with care, and I do because I want to. Just like you, I only have a limited amount of time on this earth, and I don't want to spend my time doing things that don't bring me joy. That's why I chose this path—seeing other people work towards their own financial freedom gives me joy and makes my life more joyful.

It's that bond that's more than just a transaction, that's why I am in this business. When I have clients, grown men, fathers and grandfathers who have made it through life with grit and hard work come in, I can see them relax once they see their plan come to life.

Retirees that can't know how much money they will have to spend above their monthly bills won't feel free to spend on the things they want, which is why the creation of these income streams that can always be relied upon is an important consideration in this journey. Peace of mind may sound like a New Age concept that is hard to define, but it has deep roots in our psychological survival instincts. Many people who thought to save enough for retirement will not spend outside of their means, so if their means are certain and stable, the ability to spend will be stable, and if income is unstable, you might not feel safe going out for that dinner or taking that weekend trip to see the grandkids.

And it's not just about spending ability either, it's about weathering the vicissitudes of the economic and political landscape that seems so supercharged with volatility over the past two decades. Many people think that you just have to tolerate this, that risk is always high and the market has to have a significant impact on your month-to-month income in retirement, but that's just not true. Again, it is heavily dependent on the assets and goals of each retiree, but once we settle on how to create a plan that provides you with the guaranteed income you need, that is where the ability to have peace of mind begins. It is where we plant the seed of personal freedom.

And what grows out of that seed is different for every retiree. Sometimes it's easy to visualize, and sometimes it's hard, but that's where my approach really kicks in to do the heavy lifting. Many clients run into situations they didn't envision and indeed end up having a very hard time visualizing what that freedom looks like in a situation they hadn't imagined.

NEXT UP

Congratulations on setting yourself up to reap the benefits of all the hard work, sweat and tears. Those long hours and weeks have set you up to live the life that only you can dream of. It's time to take that first step, to plant the seed and watch that garden grow, the one that allows you to cultivate the beautiful and meaningful things that life offers. It's time to start that journey, for yourself and your loved ones, and I'll be here the whole time to help you see that dream into the world.

In our last chapter, Chapter 11, you'll learn what you can do to help set your dream retirement into motion.

11

EMBARK UPON YOUR RETIREMENT JOURNEY

What I have laid out for you in this book is a philosophy. It's not about numbers and spreadsheets—sure, those are important, and here more so than other places—but make no mistake, at the end of the day this is about you and your dreams. A retirement plan, just like a fingerprint, must be unique. And the sooner you get started mapping that plan, the more likely you are to live in a reality that translates your dreams into the retirement you've always desired.

Whether you have thought deeply about those dreams or not given them another glance during your waking hours, the time to act is now. And it's not about taking any action, it's about taking the right action. You've probably heard the saying: A failure to plan is a plan to fail. Without appropriate planning, you may not be able to turn your dream retirement into a reality. I would ask: What are you waiting for?

That process can start right now, right where you are sitting and reading this, all you have to do is get in touch to start the journey. Consider that when you take action to realize your retirement dreams, you aren't just acting for yourself. You are taking responsibility for your future. You are preparing a legacy that can financially, emotionally and spiritually nourish your family, your descendants and your community. You are committing yourself to maximizing the resources that you have worked so hard to save.

My vision for you and countless others—is more than financial planning. It's a movement built on the belief that you deserve nothing less than the retirement you've always imagined.

What moves me most about this work is witnessing transformation: watching clients evolve from rough sketches of retirement dreams into people living those dreams fully. This journey isn't just about reaching the destination—every step along the way deserves to be treasured.

Creating your retirement plan early isn't merely practical: It's foundational. It becomes your North Star, your commitment to yourself. And I truly believe this: Developing that plan as part of a dedicated team feels infinitely better than navigating alone.

Going at this alone might mean betting that you can master what skilled professionals spend decades learning—and could be a risky gamble with your future. Instead, picture yourself with a trusted partner by your side, someone who not only supports your vision but helps adapt your plan as life unfolds. Because your retirement will evolve, the economy will shift, and circumstances will change.

We can't predict what tomorrow brings, so why add unnecessary uncertainty to one of life's most important transitions?

Take a deep breath. Trust the process. Let's embark on this journey together.

Among my clients are a group of doctors, who have a hard job that's only getting harder. Some of them are retiring early, due to declining reimbursements or increasing documentation demands from electronic health records. Let's take another fictional example culled from the types of clients I deal with frequently. Dr. L is retiring because the demands of corporate healthcare, electronic medical records and more, mean that he has less time to spend with his patients than ever before. It used to be that he would see 20 patients a day, and have time to spend with them, build relationships and monitor their health in the way that he felt best. When his practice was bought by a hospital, his patient load increased, as did the amount of documentation for patient care that he needed to provide. Over time, insurance company documentation, including pre-authorizations and insurance company denials, was consuming more of his time.

"I went to medical school so I could help people," he confided. "Not so I could spend most of my time on the computer or on the phone with insurance companies." People like Dr. L have made me realize how fortunate I am because I can spend as much time with my clients as they need. My job is special for many reasons, but one reason is because I have a duty to offer advice that is in the best interest of my clients. I'm not beholden to anything more than that. That's where this philosophy grows from, this duty is a bond to my clients. That bond, the one I take so seriously, is what led me to the conclusion that a retirement plan must grow out of a holistic assessment. There are no shortcuts, no one-size-fits-all solutions here. Yes, I have general principles I prefer because they are evidence-based, but that is only part of the framework we are building this dream on.

CREATE THE BEST OPPORTUNITY FOR RETIREMENT SUCCESS

I'm not one to repeat myself more than I need to, but I'm afraid that I often need to repeat what I'm about to say, and it's going to sound familiar because I just alluded to it earlier in this chapter. The skills needed to save and invest for retirement differ significantly from those necessary to create and manage a retirement income plan once you've retired. For one, actual saving is more than half the battle when saving for retirement. By that, I mean the discipline to keep saving for retirement even when you had to shortchange your life-style to save at the right level. Not everyone has the discipline to save, and saving is what really creates the foundation for a successful retirement. Investing for retirement is not as complex as you might think because company 401(k) plans only offer so many options and those options are typically oriented towards capital appreciation, because you want your retirement assets to grow. However, because you only have one chance to retire right, you need to give yourself—and your family—the best possible chance to succeed.

You have been good about saving for retirement and that is something to be celebrated. But that is the beginning of a process, not the end. So even earlier than the savings phase, it's good to start considering the options. You don't have to commit to an advisor as a 20-year-old, but starting early to consider your future needs can help improve your results. Life is busy enough as it is, switching jobs, moving to a house, all these major life events that are a hassle to accomplish also have ramifications for your financial future. So don't be afraid to get in touch early, especially because the money that grows the most is often the money that was saved early and invested well. Through early planning and the disciplined implementation of financial knowledge, some people could retire as early as age 45, 50, or 55, rather than waiting until the conventional retirement age of 65.

Nobody wants to be swamped with unforeseen expenses going into the stretch run of your career. In my experience, there are so many crucial aspects that go under-appreciated during early retirement planning. It's not just about income, although that certainly is the most crucial factor. It encompasses healthcare, Social Security, housing, taxation, and estate planning, each requiring separate attention while remaining interconnected.

Many financial advisors emphasize returns—but returns are far from the only factor that matters in retirement income planning. You may think that one financial advisor is as good as the next. But the reality is that because there is only one chance per life to retire, it does come down to finding that one right person who is going to meet you where you are and figure out with you where you want to go. I believe that that person is me!

And just like I tell my clients, if you aren't sure about whether you're on the right path with your current retirement plan or your financial advisor, then go get a second opinion. A second opinion can be just as important for retirement as in medicine. When you go to get that second opinion, I recommend getting personal with your questions, to really get to know the person who is going to be handling your money, going to be responsible for your future and your family's future. One question that tends to be a great gauge for people is whether your financial advisor has a financial advisor of their own. I advise and I am a resource to other financial advisors. Just like a doctor shouldn't be their own doctor, an advisor shouldn't be their own advisor.

Most advisors have strong beliefs about systems and frameworks and a wealth of information many other retirees don't have, but at the end of the day we can only know what we know, so having another objective source of information can be a counterweight to all of the time we spend in the office thinking about other people, and it allows us to bring insights about our own financial wellbeing to our clients.

Our comprehensive team of retirement advisors, CPAs, hedge fund advisors, and advanced planning professionals provides a thorough process and extensive guidance for prospective clients who want a fresh perspective on retirement planning. The sooner we get started the better, but there is no obligation because we know the value of what we are offering will make it clear to those who are looking.

My goal is to build stable, strong and fulfilling relationships with my clients that will stand the test of a 20, 25, 30 year—or longer retirement. That relationship needs to be sustained over good markets, and bad, strong economies and recessions, the best events of your retirement—and, at times, the worst.

This is where the world and finances meet pertaining to what I call the influence of money. There certainly has been a financial market evolution over the last decades. Our team's collective experience helps us understand where the industry has been and where it's heading This is how our experience stands out from other financial advisors to help meet the needs for early, traditional and late retirement.

While most of the time that I spend with my clients is happy and warm, I have spent time with people I care about at their lowest moments. My job is to build them up and to offer real hope, not smoke and mirrors, but the genuine article.

For example, consider the hypothetical story of George and

Amara. George died after a debilitating stroke and it took Amara years to recover to the point where she could enjoy her life, family and grandchildren again. To reclaim her life took incredible courage, but sometimes it's the caregiver that predeceases the cared for. I've seen situations where the spouse that was cared for then has to enter a facility; proper planning will ensure that at least this isn't a financial burden. Otherwise, there is the chance that retirees won't be able to go out and enjoy themselves in any part of the world they wish or are restricted from doing the hobbies they plan to enjoy in retirement. Not only that, but they may face bills they hadn't dreamed of since they believed they would be the one to go first, and that the math would ease up on their partner afterwards. It's a hard task for anyone involved in that situation to be dealing with this new and unexpected reality. But that's when the rubber really hits the road. My job is to be here during the good and tough times.

THE BEAUTY OF TAKING ACTION

Outside of work I love to host and entertain. It's about letting other people know that you love them and care for them. To do it right you need to know who is eating the food. To know the things that make them unique. To tailor a spread, a dish to their particular tastes and their wants. You almost have to know them better than they know themselves if you want to do the best job possible. I'm good at that.

When I think about making a plan for someone, it's a lot like when I think about who is coming to my dining room table on the holidays or any other time. The main difference is that when I take my apron off and head to the office, you have my complete and total attention. The plan we make doesn't have to suit anyone else's shared tastes, it's all for you.

We do only get one chance to set that table, sit down and dig in thoroughly when we talk about retirement. People don't want good enough when they retire, they want optimal. I say that from so many years of experience. Sometimes retirees come to me from a previous advisor or no retirement guidance, and we have to switch it up halfway through their golden years. The way to avoid that is simple. Come and talk to me, and we can get started.

EPILOGUE

This poem was written by my mother, Linda Craig Sullivan, before her passing. It shares her thoughts about how life is beautiful in all phases. I hope you enjoy her wisdom as much as I do.

How to Make a Beautiful Life

Love yourself.
Make peace with who you are.
And where you are,
at this moment in time.

Listen to your heart.
If you can hear what it's saying,
in this noisy world.

Make time for yourself.
Enjoy your own company.
Let your mind wander among the stars.

Take chances.
Make mistakes.

Life can be messy,
and confusing a times,
but its also full of surprises.
The next rock in the path,
might be a stepping stone.

"Be Happy,"
when you don't have what you want.
Want what you have.
Make do.
That's a well-kept secret of contentment.

There aren't any short cuts to tomorrow.
You have to make your own way.
To know where you're going,
is only part of it.

You need to know where you've been too.
And if you ever get lost,
don't worry.

The people who love you will find you.
Count on it.

Life isn't days and years,
it's what you do with time.
And with all the goodness and grace,
that's inside you,
Make A Beautiful Life,
the kind of life you deserve.

ACKNOWLEDGMENTS

I've had professional inspirations for this book over 30 years ago, stemming from my family's retirement planning, which has evolved into life, income, and legacy planning for my immediate family and clients. From a leadership perspective, I believe my mentor and other professionals (including my publishing team) have served as sources of inspiration. Thus, *The Season of Yes* was born.

As I express my gratitude for completing this work, I must start with my Lord and Savior. "To whom much is given; much is required" is my daily mantra.

I thank my dear husband, Dr. Carlos J. Littlejohn, who gently but effectively nudges me to write with an educational focus, as the overall goal is to teach others how to strategically and effectively manage their financial wealth. Thank you for your unwavering support and encouragement throughout the entire process.

To my *legacy*, my children, Markeith-Dakarai Douglas, Dyamond-Marai Douglas, and Carlos "Two" Littlejohn II, and my grandchildren, Nasir and Sevn-Amari, thank you for your patience and for giving me the drive to complete this work so I may be a "watch tower to the world." I hope this accomplishment inspires you to be intentional in your pursuit of greatness and to go beyond limits. To my siblings, family members, trusted circle of colleagues and friends, thank you for the ongoing encouragement, celebratory moments, and checking on me throughout the process of this work.

To my avid clients and readers of *The Season of Yes*, thank you for investing in me and allowing me to guide you through a comprehensive and holistic approach to retirement. I hope this book provides insight to share "pearls of wisdom" and teaching moments. This book would not have happened without you.

ABOUT THE AUTHOR

"I'm here to help you uncover your financial priorities, plan for the future, and live your best life"

M. Felicia Douglas Littlejohn is an award-winning Investment Advisor Representative and Principal of Legacy Financial Advisors. She's also a licensed insurance agent and National Social Security Advisor (NSSA®) designee. Her core services include Retirement Income Strategies, Social Security Maximization, and Wealth Management. She has been serving clients and retirees for 20-plus years, successfully establishing herself as a resource in South Carolina, Georgia, and North Carolina. She earned a Top Advisor Award for her 2023 total annuity production from CreativeOne.

Felicia services private and public institutions, business owners, pre-retirees, retirees, and other individuals by delivering client-centered and priority-driven financial strategies at her offices located in the Greenville and Anderson areas.

As a testament to her unwavering commitment to her career and community, she has received several commendations from various organizations for her civic and philanthropic efforts in promoting economic development and financial empowerment.

To learn more, please visit: www.thelegacygroupsolutions.com

www.ingramcontent.com/pod-product-compliance
Lightning Source LLC
Chambersburg PA
CBHW041259210926
51847CB00009B/76
9781954624412